Strategies for Mentoring

Strategies for Mentoring

A Blueprint for Successful Organizational Development

Christopher Conway

JOHN WILEY & SONS
Chichester • New York • Weinheim • Brisbane • Singapore • Toronto

Copyright © 1998 by Christopher Conway

Published 1998 by John Wiley & Sons Ltd,
             Baffins Lane, Chichester,
             West Sussex PO19 1UD, England

                 National   01243 779777
                 International   (+44) 1243 779777

             e-mail (for orders and customer service enquiries): cs-books@wiley.co.uk
             Visit our Home Page on http://www.wiley.co.uk
                           or http://www.wiley.com

All Rights Reserved. No part of this publication may be reproduced, stored in a retrieval system, or transmitted, in any form or by any means, electronic, mechanical, photocopying, recording, scanning or otherwise, except under the terms of the Copyright, Designs and Patents Act 1988 or under the terms of a licence issued by the Copyright Licensing Agency, 90 Tottenham Court Road, London W1P 9HE, UK, without the permission in writing of the copyright owner.

Other Wiley Editorial Offices

John Wiley & Sons Inc., 605 Third Avenue,
New York, NY 10158-0012, USA

WILEY-VCH Verlag GmbH, Pappelallee 3,
D-69469 Weinheim, Germany

Jacaranda Wiley Ltd, 33 Park Road, Milton,
Queensland 4064, Australia

John Wiley & Sons (Asia) Pte Ltd, 2 Clementi Loop #02-01,
Jin Xing Distripark, Singapore 129809

John Wiley & Sons (Canada) Ltd, 22 Worcester Road,
Rexdale, Ontario M9W 1L1, Canada

British Library Cataloguing in Publication Data

A catalogue record for this book is available from the British Library

ISBN 0 471 984388

Typeset in 11/13pt Palatino by Footnote Graphics, Warminster, Wiltshire.
Printed and bound in Great Britain by Biddles Ltd, Guildford and King's Lynn.
This book is printed on acid-free paper responsibly manufactured from sustainable forestation, for which at least two trees are planted for each one used in paper production.

For my parents
Vanessa and Arthur Conway

Contents

Foreword and Acknowledgements		ix
1	Mentoring—Management or Organization Development?	1
2	Mentoring in Organizations	9
3	Implementing Mentoring in the Organization	27
4	Mentoring and Training and Development	39
5	Mentoring and Developing High Flyers	59
6	Mentoring and Building Diversity in Organizations	79
7	Mentoring and Graduate Development	101
8	Mentoring and Change	113
9	The Role of Mentoring in Developing Global Managers and Organizations	129
10	The Impact of Cultural Differences on International Mentoring	153
11	Implementing Mentoring Internationally	181
Bibliography and Further Reading		185
Index		193

Foreword and Acknowledgements

This book is the fruit of an interest in mentoring which has extended back over nearly a decade. It has been informed by research, consultancy and debate with like-minded people from many different organizations, cultures and backgrounds. It concentrates on mentoring in its strategic application to organizations and does not attempt to cover mentoring in all its many other uses. It is intended to be a highly practical guide for managers who are interested in how they might use mentoring to benefit the development of their organizations and the individuals within them.

I am deeply grateful to my friend and collaborator Kevin Barham, Director of the Ashridge Centre for Research into Management and Organization Development, for permission to reproduce much of a report on international mentoring which we wrote under the auspices of the Centre as well as other Ashridge reports. He is my co-author in respect of the chapters on international mentoring.

I should also like to thank Michael Osbaldeston, Chief Executive of Ashridge, for his support and encouragement of our work in the field of international mentoring, as well as other colleagues at Ashridge too numerous to name—they know who they are.

My gratitude is also due to the organizations which have been named in this book. I should like to thank particularly Beth Cape, Head of Management Development at LIFFE; Lianne Hornsey, Vice President, Europe BMG; Sharon Docherty, KMDS Manager, Kingfisher; Arne Brinkman, Vice President, HR, Stora; Guy Halliwell of Brent; and Janet King, HR Director of Frimley Park NHS Hospital Trust. Without their cooperation this book would not have been possible.

I hope that this book will be a timely and above all practical contribution to the needs of those facing the decision of whether or not to use mentoring as part of the development processes of their organizations.

Chapter 1

Mentoring—Management or Organization Development?

Mentoring has had a varied history in organizational life. It seems to have gone through several stages. These stages form a kind of evolutionary scale for many individuals. Where people in organizations become aware of what may be a mentoring relationship (and often they do not), it is sometimes seen as unusual and there may be a hostile reaction. Once any gossip of a personal nature ('it must be an affair—his poor wife') has been eliminated, albeit reluctantly, the grapevine concludes that the relationship under scrutiny represents some form of patronage and therefore by definition is exclusionary to others in the organization. This is seen as favouritism and therefore unfair. It is possible for the two parties to the relationship to face pressure from the organization to end their 'unusual' activities, unless of course they hold very senior positions in the company.

There was a time when mentoring could have been seen as a way of replicating the existing management profile to the exclusion of others. It is a tribute to the flexibility and innate strength of mentoring that it has lost this image and has been adopted as a powerful tool in building the diverse organization.

The alternative view of a mentoring relationship may be 'well, it must be a performance issue' and the attention an individual is receiving is remedial in nature—a bit of extra coaching. This may cause further jealousies—why her or him? Once more, this may be perceived as unfair and, as we know, perceptions are very important in organizations. This interpretation can also devalue the concept of mentoring as being useful only for the failures. Rarely does the organizational grapevine recognize the full potential of mentoring.

The next stage of evolution may be that some senior individuals in the organization, usually prompted by considerations of management succession and retention of high-performing and high-potential individuals, light on mentoring—often the chief executive has read about it in the management section of the in-flight magazine. He (it often still is) decides that he and several senior directors are good sorts and would make excellent mentors. Once on land, he sends a memo to his top cadre announcing his decision and suggesting that they should get some protégés. They need no further encouragement—this could win them 'brownie points' with the boss as well as giving an opportunity to poach a few 'bright' people and build a good team around themselves. Besides, they *know* that they would make marvellous mentors. The only worry at this stage is to make sure of getting the right people—no one likes second choice and no one wants a 'turkey' for a protégé. Unkind maybe, but this view has been known to prevail.

Unfortunately, the way in which this approach is implemented means that no one discusses the business case for mentoring in any depth, the mentors receive no development and do not share ideas on what mentoring is about in their organization and what they should be doing. There are no checks or safeguards in place and then when the initiative hits the high-potential people selected, it resembles a bolt from the blue. The chief executive is perplexed when the attrition rate is still the same as it was and the competitors are still poaching good people. Why? The answer is easy to guess. The approach is *ad hoc* and uncoordinated and, even if we dispense with the word protégé, it still smacks of patronage rather than mentoring. Even if there are some successes, the problem remains that an individual or a few individuals may have developed—a management development approach—but maybe at a disproportionate cost to the organization itself. This élitist approach can alienate people and cost too much in wasted management time.

So can we use mentoring to develop people in organizations without these costs? The final stage of evolution of mentoring is a strategic organizational development approach. Until this point, mentoring has been viewed as a management development tool more akin to the training and development ethos of most organizations. It is regarded as personal development that benefits individuals primarily and only incidentally, perhaps, the organization itself. Unfortunately, this approach has been confused with counselling and has led to mentoring being seen as 'pink and fluffy'—or a concept that revolves around personal support and hence is not directly related to more general business needs.

What is now proposed is an approach called *organizational mentoring*. What is this and how can it benefit organizations? Can it benefit organizations across all sectors of the economy?

In researching this idea, we have to understand the concept and dynamics of mentoring and test the hypothesis that this could be replicated in the organizational context. Having done this, it becomes necessary to observe certain guidelines to ensure the successful implementation of the concept. Research and consultancy have shown that this can be done and that there is no one type of organizational culture which can grow mentoring—it can thrive anywhere. It will, of course, be perceived and implemented differently in diverse cultures.

A STRATEGIC APPROACH

The first premise of organizational mentoring is that we are building a strategic organizational approach.

Why do we do anything in an organization? Surely, the answer is to ensure its competitiveness. This can be measured in many different ways. Charities, commercial organizations and government departments have their own missions, values and visions for achieving success, but all are competing for resources and success on their own terms.

We can illustrate the strategic place of mentoring in organizations by using the model in Figure 1.1. In many organizations, top management spend a great deal of time working out the vision and strategy and striving for this to be communicated effectively further down the organization. They are concerned with the management skills or management competencies that are necessary to achieve the organizational mission.

Management style is often one of the most neglected and potentially most powerful contributory factors to competitive success. Management style comprises not just how offices are organized (open plan or individual offices) or how people prefer to communicate (by e-mail, telephone or face to face), but most importantly how we treat each other and how people manage or lead themselves and others. This is really governed by the corporate values. Values in this context are not handy wishlists that can be produced for public consumption, but

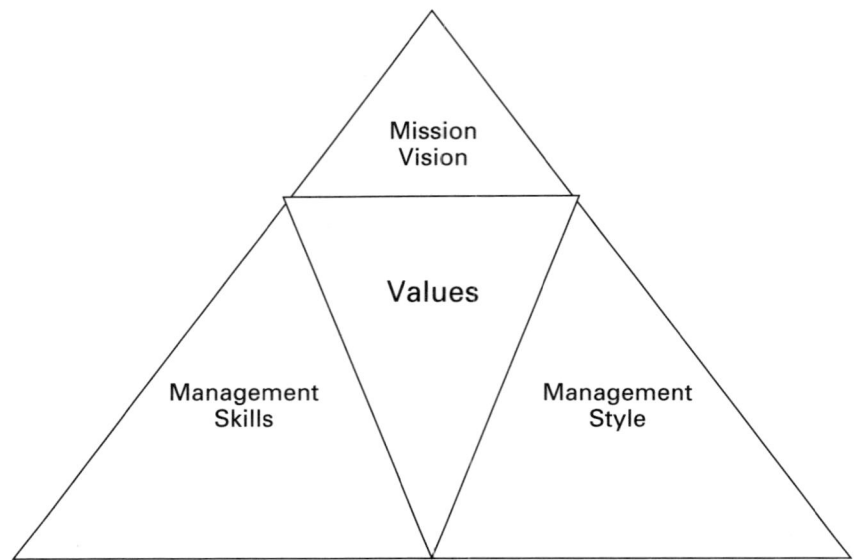

Figure 1.1 The Core of the New Organization

rather what underlies the collective behaviour of the people in the organization. This is true also for the other segments of the model, but especially so for management style. It is within management style that organizational mentoring can be placed.

Mentoring schemes are important to get mentoring itself off to a good start. However, when we implement mentoring effectively in the organizational context, we are really implementing *change*. Mentoring on its own does not bring about change, but used in conjunction with other approaches it can be a powerful contributory agent of change.

So how could mentoring contribute to the competitiveness agenda of your organization and add value? As we shall see, there are several issues to be addressed before implementing a mentoring initiative.

MENTORING—A PANACEA?

Mentoring alone is not going to solve all your management and organizational problems. Indeed, alone it achieves very little and may actually harm morale by allowing disaffected people to collude without an agenda, which could deteriorate into 'whinging' to one another.

Organizational mentoring has to have a focus, a valid reason in order to gain support and engender clarity of purpose among participants.

Mentoring works best in conjunction with other approaches such as management succession planning and a strategic competency initiative. It can also support development workshops and performance management systems.

BUSINESS CASE

Can you state your business case cogently? Is it to assist in the development of graduates or for high flyers? Or is it to assist in developing global managers? What is mentoring going to support? This must be clear in order to achieve success and to get top management on board quickly and enthusiastically.

DEFINING MENTORING FOR YOUR ORGANIZATION

Copying others on this one is out! Good ideas travel, but mentoring must be done by the organization for itself. When we examine definitions, we shall see that there are many different types of mentoring. It is important to know exactly what you mean by mentoring and if that works for your organization then it represents success. It is easy to become 'hung up' on definitions, but in this case it is important to distinguish mentoring from other support relationships. It is rather like the old adage: 'we need to know the rules if we are going to break them'.

LEARNING AND MENTORING

We talk a lot about the learning organization, but it is still worth repeating that it is people who learn, and usually from each other. Traditionally, 'quality' learning has often been perceived as being undertaken in a formal, classroom or business school environment. There is a move today towards understanding that, as Aristotle put it, 'what we learn, we learn by doing'; without diminishing Aristotle's contribution, we might add: 'and by asking someone about it'. But who can we ask?

6   MENTORING—MANAGEMENT OR ORGANIZATION DEVELOPMENT

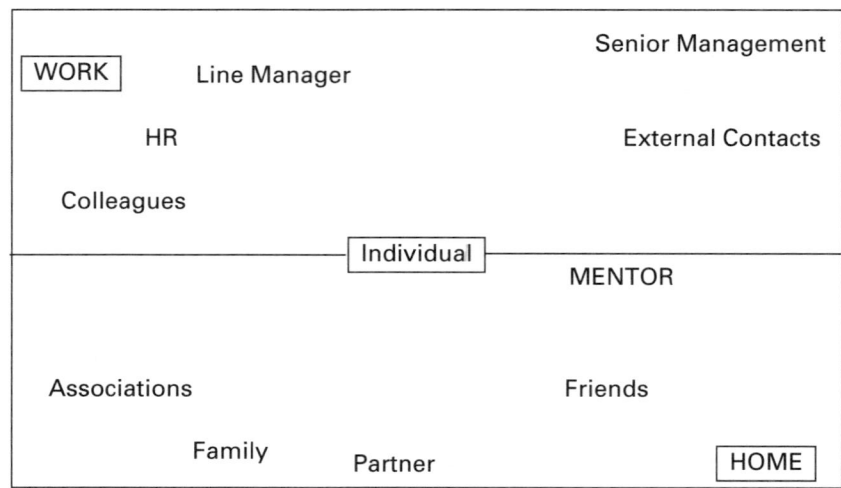

Figure 1.2   The Learning Universe

Figure 1.2 endeavours to show that we are not alone in the learning universe. The whole shift in organizations to enabling individuals to take control of their own development has resulted in people looking around to find out where they can obtain the help necessary to succeed. We can ask for certain things from our boss, from our HR colleagues and maybe from senior management. However, there are times when we need to be challenged, supported and to enquire in an environment that can provide criticism and positive feedback without a potentially negative agenda driving it. This is often provided by family and friends, sometimes by acquaintances but always as an ideal by a mentor.

The mentor's position on the line between home and work illustrates that the mentor *may* be in a better position than other colleagues to see and appreciate both sides of your life. A mentor within the same organization has the advantage of being ideally suited to understanding and operating within that organization. However, mentors who are external to your organization can play a valuable role too. Whom you use as a mentor is directly related to the purpose of your mentoring initiative. When looking for answers to questions about implementing mentoring, go back to basics and ask: 'why are we doing this, what is the purpose of our mentoring?' The answers are usually clearer in this context.

The concept of organizational mentoring is grounded in the belief that it is a complementary approach that must be used as part of a wider strategy to achieve excellence in corporate development. Like any other serious strategic intervention, organizational mentoring needs to be treated with respect and, when evaluated, should amply repay the resources committed to it—provided that its aims are clear and unambiguous and communicated to those involved.

Chapter 2

Mentoring in Organizations

Mentoring is one of the fastest-growing trends in management in the UK. So what is it and why are business organizations using it to develop their management? From research into this area over the last five years, it is possible to say that there is an increasing interest in and use of mentoring for a variety of different business cases. Recent surveys indicate that up to half of UK and US organizations are using mentoring in one form or another. In order to replicate the mentoring relationship in organizations (and it is a *relationship*, not an activity or process), great care has to be taken in designing the mechanics of the mentoring approach.

We have developed a new approach, called the *Mentoring Contract*, that helps to manage the expectations of mentors, mentorees and the organization itself. The 'contract' is an informal, verbal agreement between the mentor and the mentoree that sets out their expectations for the mentoring relationship at the start.

Mentoring is used in a variety of ways in organizations: to develop high-potential managers and new graduate entrants, to assist in developing international managers and even directors, to contribute to qualification programmes, to help build the diverse organization and to foster the management of change. It is this last point that helps position mentoring as a strategic organization development tool as well as a management development intervention. Mentoring at its most effective is about helping to change the management style and culture of an organization and positively contributing to competitive edge.

Among a wide variety of applications, mentoring does the following:

- helps induct new staff more quickly
- improves recruitment and retention of key people

- assists in identifying potential more effectively
- helps in identifying key competencies
- encourages diversity in the workplace
- helps in the speedy absorption of new entrants
- gives recruitment and retention benefits
- aids improved organizational communication
- enhances the transfer of skills
- improves leadership and management succession
- improves productivity
- is a cost-effective development method
- can enhance competitive edge
- can be a stabilizing factor in times of corporate change
- develops global managers

The following case studies illustrate some of these different business cases.

British Alcan uses mentoring for graduate, young, high-potential managers, some senior managers and to support an MBA programme. In the graduate scheme, there has been a deliberate policy of linking very senior management with the graduate group. This flies in the face of the policy of not linking people where there is too much of an experience gap. The reasoning behind this approach is to facilitate induction and to assess the potential of the graduate group informally and over time. Both the mentors and mentees (as they are called in British Alcan) have found that the differential levels have benefited their relationships, which are conducted in a relaxed way.

LIFFE (London International Financial Futures and Options Exchange) uses mentoring for its high-potential graduate entrants. The mentorees are linked with people at head of department or director level for a period of one year. The purpose of the mentoring scheme is to underpin the career development of these young people and help the Exchange to retain valuable people in the competitive environment of the City. Over the last two years since the mentoring scheme has been in place, LIFFE has achieved this objective and is looking at ways in which the benefits of mentoring may be extended throughout the organization.

A major financial services institution used exclusively dedicated external consultants to support the entire management population through a programme of major change. The mentoring programme, a two-year project, was designed as part of a comprehensive approach to change management. One of the objectives was to enable the mentees to become effective mentors themselves, so that the mentoring philosophy and process becomes the primary leadership style of the organization.

Brent Council, already known for its leadership in encouraging women in management, has used mentoring to help the development of women middle managers into more senior roles. The results of a post-reorganization audit in 1992 showed that only 11% of senior managers were women, despite their being 65% of the workforce. To help remedy this situation, a mentoring scheme was devised exclusively for women middle managers. The Council felt that research and practical experience have shown that when men are encouraged to act as mentors to women on a formal basis, this can help women to break down some of the barriers that deter their progress and assist them in moving on and upwards in their career development.

Trafalgar House Construction has used mentoring to support its own 'in-house' MBA programme. The basis for mentoring here is to support high-potential managers who are candidates on an internal MBA programme, which in turn supports a proactive management succession strategy. It was felt that managers on the programme were already leading pressured work lives and a means of supporting them was sought that would help them cope with the extra pressures. This had to be achieved without stimulating accusations of reliance or favouritism in a fairly 'self-help', not to say rather 'macho', organizational culture. Also, it was felt that using mentors would assist mentorees (called associates) to focus their learning back in the workplace and share with others not on the programme. This approach helps to deflect accusations of élitism.

At *X Bank*, mentoring underpins many aspects of the management development process. One of the main challenges in introducing self-managed learning is how to ensure that what is learned by an individual is supported, reinforced and shared in the workplace. One support identified by the company was mentoring. However, there were several other reasons for introducing mentoring:

- to help inculcate a cross-functional approach to management—using mentoring as an organizational development strategy;

- to help develop a trusting and sharing culture at senior levels of the organization;
- to assist in career development and succession planning.

Thus, mentoring was seen in the context of supporting the whole learning strategy.

South West Thames Regional Health Authority has used mentoring in several locations to mentor clinical staff who need to adapt to the major changes taking place in the NHS. The aim of the programme was to help a group of ambitious and committed nurses (men and women) to develop skills outside their usual sphere and to extend their management experience. The programme was designed to be a positive and stimulating experience for everyone. It was aimed at breaking down occupational barriers and helping each individual in the mentoring relationship to grow both personally and professionally. Of the 20 mentoring pairs in the pilot, only one 'failed', apparently because the partners said that the mentoring process did not meet expectations. The majority found the programme valuable in extending themselves in the workplace.

STORA, a Swedish forest products group and Europe's oldest company, uses mentoring in the international context to support global integration. Mentorees are deliberately linked with mentors from different countries, cultures and functions to understand how to gain promotion in other business areas and to stimulate a wider global perspective.

Other examples are:
- Airline *SAS* uses mentoring to support managers in key overseas posts.
- *Rhone-Poulenc*, a French chemical company, insists on 'godfathers' for its *jeune sans frontières*.
- *Cable & Wireless* is a user of mentoring partly to support the 're-entry' process in global assignments and to begin to compensate for the loss of some expatriate networks.
- *ABB Sweden* encourages mentoring for all employees, not just management.
- *Royal PTT* in the Netherlands uses mentoring to support its graduate intake.

These are just a few of the organizations that are obtaining benefits from the use of mentoring—there are many more.

WHAT IS MENTORING?

Five years ago one of our research questions was: 'If we have discovered that mentoring is a complex relationship, can it be replicated by design in an organizational context?' The answer is yes, provided that the groundrules and expectations are set out and managed effectively. From our case examples, it is evident that there is no one type of organizational sector, culture or industry that benefits from using mentoring; it is an approach that can work across all of these.

Defining mentoring and hence what a mentor does is not always an easy task. What are the differences between, for example, mentors and coaches, or mentors and sponsors? What is the relationship of counselling to mentoring? Fear of having to counsel people is a deterrent to some senior managers volunteering themselves as mentors in organizations. They need reassurance that there is a difference between professional counselling and counselling as informal advice, only one of which is generally appropriate to mentoring in organizations.

Devotees of musical films will recall *My Fair Lady*, based on George Bernard Shaw's play *Pygmalion*, where a distinguished language expert wagers with his friend, Colonel Pickering, that he could pass off a Cockney flower girl as a Duchess at an embassy ball. He duly does so. At first, I regarded Professor Higgins as Eliza Doolittle's mentor. I was wrong: he was her coach. In fact, the person who was her mentor—advising, comforting, being practical about buying new clothes for her and taking a wider view of what was going on—was Colonel Pickering. Once this penny drops, the film can be seen as reflecting the dynamics of a successful mentoring, as well as coaching, relationship. It is also, incidentally, a good musical.

More and more over the last few years we have been hearing the words 'mentor' and 'mentoring' and just as often we have been given several different and even conflicting views of what constitutes the concept and mechanics of the mentoring relationship.

There is no standard definition of the word 'mentor' outside of the dictionary, which refers to Odysseus entrusting his son Telemachus to the goddess Athene, who disguised herself as Mentor (an old male friend of Odysseus). Her function, we are told by Homer, was to be a wise counsellor and helper to the youth. This situation gives rise to one or two interesting thoughts. The first is that 'mentoring' as such does not exist—it is something that Mentor, a person, did! This leads us to the core of 'mentoring', which is that once the expectations and mechanics of the processes of mentoring are agreed, there is little to do but allow people to get on with it in their own way. Each mentor and mentoring relationship is and should be different from any other in the way that it progresses. For the organization it must reflect the 'tight-loose' concept, or 'organize the expectations and structure and let people get on with it'.

The second thought is that the first mentor was a woman seeming to be a man; or, as a goddess, perhaps Athene encapsulated the virtues of both sexes equally. Maybe this illustrates that it is important that the good mentor has a balance of skills and behaviours that can be termed masculine and feminine. This thought tends to be borne out by our research, which has shown that the gender of the mentor is irrelevant to a good mentoring relationship—it is the quality of the mentor that is paramount. An exception to this is that some women, especially in mentoring schemes to promote diversity, prefer to have a female mentor. In many organizations these are in short supply. This in turn often leads to a shorter timescale for the mentoring relationship, or mentors who end up with more than one mentoree.

Our concern in this instance is to discover what a definition of organizational mentoring might look like. It has been suggested that the process is widely defined and variously named as coaching, counselling, sponsorship and apprenticeship. However, in today's new flatter and more responsive organizational environment, the mentor's role is highly specific. A mentor is an experienced, highly objective individual, who is capable of being a mirror and reflecting back to the mentoree thoughts, ideas, behaviours and situations so that the mentoree can 'stand outside the square', gain perspective and reexamine, reflect on and reprioritize their position. This sounds simple!

The role of the mentor is not about power and sponsorship or purely about age, just being older than the mentoree. The important factor in being a mentor is experience, particularly in the organizational context. It is crucial to match the mentor with the mentoree on the basis of the needs of the individuals concerned. Mentors have two central roles, to be a *support* but also to *challenge* the mentoree. Part of the strength of the mentor is not getting emotionally involved with the mentoree to the point where the advantages of perspective and objectivity are lost. Mentors must also avoid carrying the burden, fighting the battles and generally carrying the mentoree. In the organizational context, they must remember that it is their responsibility to take the long-term view for both the individual and the organization.

The following is a definition of mentoring in the organizational context:

Mentoring in organizations is a private relationship between two individuals based on a mutual desire for development towards an organizational objective. The relationship is a non-reporting one and infringes none of the organizational structures in place. It is additional to other forms of assistance, not a replacement.

If we look in more detail at this definition, we can expand some of the component parts.

'Private relationship between two individuals'

It is important that mentoring relationships are private ones. If it uses a mentoring approach, the organization is committing resources and wishes to evaluate and monitor the mentoring relationships. This is a very delicate area. If the organization 'over-polices' the mentoring scheme, then the privacy that is essential to the relationship can be jeopardized. On the other hand, the scheme managers, usually but not always the HR function, need to monitor the relationships to make sure that there are no real problems brewing and also that the mentors and mentorees are actually meeting and working towards their objectives. Confidentiality is the bedrock of any mentoring relationship and cannot be risked. So the scheme managers have a tricky task in keeping tabs on what is happening without prying into what is rightly the property of the mentoring relationship.

'Mutual desire for development'

It is important that both the mentor and the mentoree gain from the mentoring relationship. It is easy to see the benefits to a mentoree who, for example, is a young person who has recently joined an organization. However, it is just as easy to find out what the benefits are to their more experienced mentors, who may well be at director level—if you ask them! Many mentors in this position gain by hearing about the impact of the management style of the organization on new people. They can gain insights into the work of parts of the organization with which they do not come into direct contact. This can assist in organizational integration and communication. They experience more closely the challenges facing employees and the impact of senior management decisions on the organization. Also, they are able to change their own mindsets and share learning with others. Mentors also have an informal opportunity to assess the competence of others in the organization based on the information that may become available as a result of the mentoring relationship.

'Towards an organizational objective'

Mentoring benefits the mentor, mentoree and others in the wider organization (see Figure 2.1). This is where mentoring and the learning organization are linked quite powerfully. There are three aspects of learning: the learning of the mentor and how this affects their impact on the organization; the learning of the mentoree and the impact on the organization; and how the organization proactively promotes the processes of sharing learning.

As part of the process of being a mentor, individuals should be encouraged to examine in detail their own style as a manager. For senior managers this may be a rare opportunity to give thought to something that they often take for granted. Being a mentor often

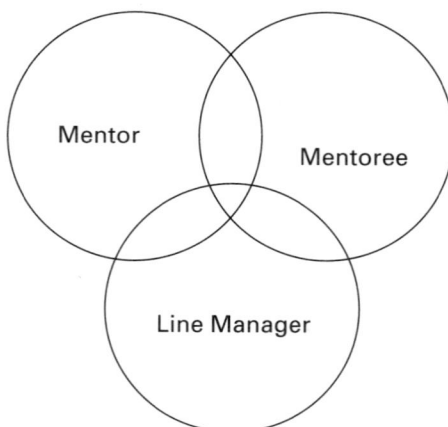

Figure 2.1 Developing the Organization and the Individual

improves the management of their own team as they take the mentor 'style' into everyday work. Mentorees often learn how to pause and take time to reflect on what they are doing and this produces improvements in management.

The organization can use mentoring relationships to stimulate organizational learning. One large company in Sweden deliberately places a manager who has newly returned to the head office with a mentoree in order that the manager/mentor can share their learning with the mentoree. The mentoree will in turn at some point get a posting abroad.

'The relationship is a non-reporting one'

As a general rule, mentors should not be in a direct line relationship with the mentoree. Mentors are usually at a tangent, in another part of the organization. This helps to relieve any sensitivities of the mentoree's line manager and provides another perspective on company affairs. It is also a good way of achieving better cross-company communication and integration. However, examples of bosses being mentors do exist, particularly in the US, and there are examples of this approach in an organization in the Czech Republic.

This may work in these cultures, but research has shown that this is not an approach to employ in the UK. Having said this, there are now companies which operate on a project basis and have abolished traditional line relationships. Many of these companies are in the high-tech sector and mentors, while not perhaps direct line managers, have in some cases taken on quasi-line-type responsibilities in regard to the mentorees. This may become the norm for companies operating in this kind of environment.

'Infringes none of the organizational structures in place'

Mentors should not have to become counsellors or disciplinarians. If a mentoree has a personal problem, it is not for the mentor to try to solve this. Obviously, advice may be offered if appropriate and if discussion of these personal matters is permitted by both parties. However, the organizational responsibilities remain with the appropriate line or function. Likewise, if the mentoree has transgressed, this again is a line matter.

'It is additional to other forms of assistance, not a replacement'

Mentoring is an extra piece of assistance. The mentor does not have to shoulder responsibilities that rightly belong with the mentoree and the line manger. This is particularly true in terms of the career development of individuals.

This is probably a good point to examine the difference between mentoring and coaching, as these two concepts sometimes get 'lumped together' in discussion and writing. One route into understanding the difference is to examine who does it. The following definition is offered:

> Coaching is more directive and focused on the job. It is a process often carried out by line managers. Mentoring is a non-directive relationship and more broadly focused. The mentor takes the longer perspective for the individual and the organization. A facilitative style is appropriate for both mentoring and coaching. Mentors can act in a coaching capacity as part of the mentoring relationship.

Mentors can coach in particular skills and the mentoring relationship may be based around this area. Some organizations, particularly in the IT field or function, use 'technical mentors' to supplement the skills coaching that is being carried out by the line. However, it is quite usual for mentoring to take place with no element of coaching. This is why valuable mentors do not have to be knowledgeable in the specialism of a mentoree. However, if a specific competency needs to be developed in a mentoree, then it may be a conscious decision to link that mentoree with a mentor who majors in that competency.

The relationship between a mentor and mentoree must always be non-directive, in the sense that learning is maximized when an individual finds their own answers. A good facilitative style is an essential part of being an effective mentor and provides the best quality of mentoring relationships.

It is possible to see a spectrum of paired support relationships, moving from Peer or Buddy, through Guide, Coach and Sponsor to Mentor (see Figure 2.2).

Peers or Buddies

These people can perform a valuable function in a variety of different ways. They can help new entrants to the organization to get settled

What is Mentoring? 19

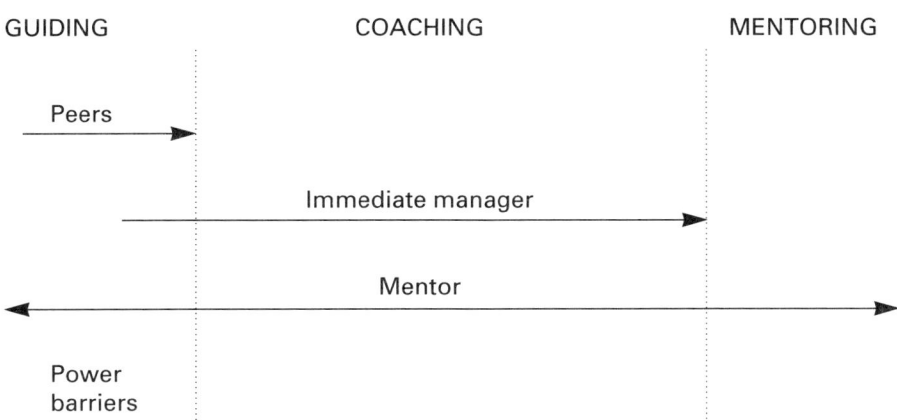

Figure 2.2 Spectrum of Paired Support Relationships

into a particular part of the organization. They can offer advice and guidance on everyday working procedures. They may be less reliable in helping the new entrant to acclimatize politically, as the buddies may not have the skills, access to information or will to achieve this. After all, it will take time to build a trusting relationship with new people, so it may be a higher-risk strategy for them to be involved in more 'political' guidance at their level in the organization.

Where buddies can be helpful is in providing a supportive and encouraging network. It is also possible to match up buddies from different parts of an organization. One company is currently considering matching up buddies from two distinct parts of the business so that they may understand each other's functions and problems better. The aim is to improve communication and integration.

Guides

Guides, although they can be buddies—there is an area of overlap—are probably part of the line function at supervisory or first-line level. Their guidance is much more likely to be job related and will overlap with coaching.

Coaches

Coaching is directly related to performance issues, is part of the overall responsibility of the line and is linked to performance management issues. The immediate line manager performs functions that encompass the guide, coach and sponsor roles. By organizational definition, the manager and those reporting to them cannot be peers (even in a 'flat' organization), or mentors in the true sense.

Sponsors

Sponsors are individuals who 'talk up' and promote the interests of the 'sponsoree'. This kind of activity can be performed by line managers who recognize the talents of their reports. Sponsoring can also be done by mentor-type figures who have the power to influence the organization. This kind of 'mentoring' still occurs naturally enough in organizations, however the function might be thought detrimental to an organizational mentoring scheme because of accusations of élitism.

Mentors

Mentors straddle all these points on the spectrum. They should have a natural, 'buddy-like' approach to their mentorees so that they can speak from a position of equality. Mentors can provide valuable guidance and can coach and sponsor if necessary. The added value is that they do not become 'stuck' in any of these roles but can move through them constantly. Mentors need, however, to achieve an element of detachment from their mentorees, in order to maximize their impact. It is important to the success of the mentoring relationship that mentors are not seen as performing an assessment role.

WHO ARE MENTORS?

A few years ago, the literature on mentoring talked about 'wise old owls'. Our research has found that age is largely irrelevant in producing excellence in a mentor. What is important is experience. This need not be in a particular function or job, but is much more about having a broad range of different experiences in different parts of an organization. This approach should produce a mentor who has a more integrated view of the business and thus is able to give a valuable overview on how change affects the whole organization.

Some academics and others have tried to produce profiles of the 'ideal' mentor (and mentoree). This approach is unnecessary and probably undesirable—one cannot clone mentors. What is desirable is to know what good mentors do and say in conducting their relationships with their mentoring partners. Good mentors come from different backgrounds and ages, but what seems to distinguish them is a belief in themselves and others and a proactive view of life. They do not wait for people to come to them—they go out looking for others.

Without being proscriptive, organizations need to be aware of some groundrules in picking mentors. Being a mentor in an organization can have consequences for the mentor. The mentor and mentoree, particularly if they have an obviously close relationship, will often be identified together. This can have positive and negative implications for how these individuals are perceived by the rest of the organization. It is important for mentors, particularly if they are very senior people, not to appear to have a 'favourite'. The behaviour of the mentoree should not seem to challenge organizational norms because they are relying on the power of the mentor. This kind of behaviour is not in the interests of the organization as a whole and can easily lead to mentoring being devalued and ultimately to fail as an élitist and 'corrupt' activity, which builds or reinforces a management 'power base'. This kind of scenario is fortunately very rare.

Selecting mentors is an important element in any organizational scheme. It is important to choose a cadre of mentors. This enables the organization to 'weed out' managers without the necessary skills or attitudes. This process is particularly important when using mentoring in a strategic way as part of the change process. However, caution is advised because the mentoring process can be used deliberately to help some of these mentors to develop. If this is the case, the mentors should be matched with mature and robust mentorees who will not be adversely affected by the developing mentor. The process almost becomes 'reverse mentoring'. In this situation, an organization should appoint a mentor for the developing mentor who can monitor and guide the approach.

Who is chosen to be a mentor will to some extent be driven by the business case and needs of the organization. The appropriateness of the gap in level and experience between the mentor and mentoree is important here. Mentors are in short supply at senior level in most organizations and there is a school of thought that says that they should not be 'wasted' on staff who are too junior or too inexperienced to take full advantage of the benefits offered by the mentoring relationship. For example, is it a legitimate use of resources to place new graduates with directors? If you are applying a 'coaching model' of mentoring, perhaps about improving skills, then the answer is clearly no. However, if you wish to show the graduates how much the organization values them, then the answer may be yes. The advantages of this approach are increased understanding for the directors of the impact of the organization's management style at this level, coupled with an opportunity to make an informal and personal evaluation of the cadre of young talent that they have recruited. Graduates make high-level contact quickly and have an opportunity to gain an overall picture of what is happening in the organization, unclouded by the perspective of one business or function. This kind of mentoring often improves the retention of high-potential graduates.

High-potential managers are usually matched with mentors at a senior level in the company. Their behaviour and how they are perceived is important for mentors. The mentorees will be successful managers in their own right with the potential to succeed senior management. Managing this type of mentoring scheme can be difficult for the human resources managers involved in its design. There are two main challenges to overcome. High-potential development can be seen as élitist and can be divisive in achieving a flatter, team-based, cooperative style of operation. Secondly, the organization may not want to indicate to the mentorees that they are on a fast track or form a special group. A way of avoiding this is to create a group of mentorees with a mixture of high potentials and others who may be high potentials in the future. Another strategy is to create several different pilot mentoring schemes for different business reasons, of which the high-potential scheme is only one. Mentors need to be briefed carefully to avoid the wrong messages being given to the high-potential group.

Mentoring replicates itself. Those people who have a mentor very often become mentors themselves. When this begins to happen, then the organization as a whole is beginning to experience a change in its culture and management style. One of the effects of mentoring is on the management style of the mentors themselves. Many mentors say that because of their experience as a mentor they treat their own reports and team differently, adopting a 'mentoring style' with them.

The selection of mentors may not be difficult, but persuading busy senior people to become mentors may seem a challenge. My work with companies has indicated two things: first, busy and successful people always find time for 'extra' important things and mentoring should be seen as a strategic organizational development initiative. Secondly, even top managers are flattered to be asked to be mentors in their organizations. Do not underestimate this.

This brings us to the question of the relationship between mentoring and role modelling. Mentors do not have to be role models and many individuals and organizations will naturally not want them to be so. Mentoring is about releasing the potential of individuals, not about cloning or copying. Respect on both sides has to be the mainstay of the mentoring relationship to achieve success.

MATCHING MENTORS AND MENTOREES

The matching process is important in creating a successful mentoring initiative. At the outset, it should be said that there is no scientific or pseudo-scientific method of matching individuals in the mentoring relationship. The basis for the matching process should reflect the business case for the mentoring scheme. If problems appear, it is wise to keep this basis at the forefront.

The 'gap' in organizational level or seniority is an important consideration. In the case of mentoring for high flyers, senior executives/ directors will be required. But do you need these people for new graduate entrants, for example? The answer depends on the business case and aim of the mentoring scheme. If one is using a coaching-type model of mentoring, where some skills coaching is evident, then the answer is probably not. That type of function can be supplied effectively by management at a lower level in the organization. However, if one is seeking to induct high-potential graduate entrants, then there are several advantages in using senior people as mentors. The graduates feel valued and their expectations of contact with senior management in the organization are met. They also feel that they have a mentor who is in a position to influence in the last resort if things are not going well—though many graduates express a view that they do not want the mentor to solve their problems for them. Indeed, this is detrimental to good mentoring practice and can cause problems with the organization's line management reporting structures.

Mentoring should not set up an alternative line reporting relationship. In addition, there are sensitivities for mentorees' line managers in the mentoring relationship. They may be suspicious and threatened by their report having contact with very senior people in the organization. The mentoree in particular must be aware of this and do nothing to inflame those potential feelings. The mentor should also be sensitive. For example, where they are visiting a graduate in the work location, they should give notice to the line management of their intentions.

Senior managers are often keen to become mentors. They often feel that it enhances others' perceptions of them and they get an opportunity to assess personally and privately the quality of the new entrants. However, it must be stressed that assessment in any formal way plays no part in a true mentoring relationship. Having said this, several organizations, notably in the IT industry, are experimenting with using mentors in this way. Their reasons are interesting. Many organizations in this sector have effectively become almost totally project based, with individuals moving from one project to another in a constant turnover of work. They are thus working for a variety of ever-changing project leaders. Add to this the fact that many of these organizations have effectively abolished their line structures and there is an organizational gap where the line manager used to be. For many working in this environment a mentor can provide the only constant in their organizational lives. The mentor will be aware of what is happening to the individual and will be in the best position, given the organizational structure, to help with the responsibilities of career development and performance appraisal.

In a recent evaluation carried out among graduates in a large organization with different constituent cultures, some mentorees expressed doubts about how suitable very senior people are to be mentors. Many said that they felt inhibited from disclosing their true feelings and concerns because they were afraid of being judged by the mentor. The graduates in this example were careful to censor what was said in the mentoring relationship. They felt that their future careers could be jeopardized by the mentors' perceptions of them. Some also said the same of mentors who were drawn from the personnel or HR function. They felt that there was frequently a lack of openness in these relationships because the graduates felt that the 'wrong' opinions or behaviour could have an adverse impact on their future careers, though the mentorees felt that it was good to have high-powered mentors. This kind of situation is a factor to bear in mind when matching individuals. One potential solution may be to use other people such as recent 'past graduates' as buddies to the new entrants, to help them with the questions that they may find difficult to ask of senior people. This kind of approach also helps to inculcate a mentoring/supportive management style in the organization.

The responsibility for matching usually rests with the HR function, who tend to be managers and champions of organizational mentoring schemes. There are many different ways of matching people. For instance, it is possible to use learning styles or psychometric profiles. However, this seems unnecessarily complex and time consuming. One of the best methods uses the 'soft' information that the organization has available. Some of the most effective matches have been made according to the 'hunches' of inspired HR professionals with a good understanding of the character and background of the individuals concerned. There is nothing wrong with 'gut feelings' about people in this instance, as much of the success of a mentoring relationship depends on the 'chemistry' between individuals. Some organizations favour a 'cheese and wine' approach, where they get potential mentors and mentorees together in a room and let them pick each other. This is not an approach to be recommended. The responsibility for matching rests with the organization and this should not be avoided.

Typically in graduate mentoring schemes, neither mentors nor graduates usually desire or need an input into the matching process. In high-potential or senior manager schemes they do. However, in organizational mentoring where the organization will have a view about the development needs and possibly the match, the matching process may involve an initial or trial match and then the mentors and mentorees have to make a valid case for a change if required. This approach goes some way towards negating charges of favouritism and power-base building in the matching of senior individuals. With high-potential participants there is a greater need for awareness of previous contacts between the mentor and mentoree—they may have worked together in the past, for example. This could produce positive or negative results for the matching process.

Most mentors find that they can cope effectively with only one mentoree. However, it may be possible for mentors to have more than one partner where there is sufficient support and time for this. In some organizations, the shortage of suitable mentors has led to one mentor being linked with several mentorees. This has often happened to senior women in organizations where there has been a demand for female mentors. In most organizations this situation is seen as less than ideal. From the perspective of the mentoree, an exception may be termed 'serial mentoring', where the mentoree has a series of different mentors for different purposes or qualities, either sequentially or concurrently. This situation is by no means unusual. Some organizations use this approach when they are developing new graduate entrants and they wish to give them a wide variety of experiences. It also applies in the international context, where an international manager in an overseas location may have a mentor in the home base as well as one in the country location.

Chapter 3

Implementing Mentoring in the Organization

Successful implementation of mentoring in an organizational context involves a 'tight–loose' approach. It is essential to prepare the best possible foundations for the mentoring initiative, while at the same time allowing people to conduct the relationships in a relaxed and personal way. The concept of the mentoring relationship will be common to all; the way each mentoring pair works together will be unique to them.

Four key learning points have emerged from my research which appear crucial in implementing an organizational mentoring initiative:

- Identify the business case and aim of your mentoring scheme—people must 'buy in'.
- Top management must be believers and demonstrate that belief.
- The mechanics and structures of the scheme must be clear to all participants.
- There is no 'prescription' for implementing mentoring—culture and values are critical factors in success.

WHAT ARE WE CALLED?

The terminology you use for mentoring should be a help rather than a hindrance. Mentor is an easy word in common currency, but what do we call the other person in the mentoring relationship? The answer seems to be don't get 'hung up' on these issues. Each organization will find something suitable for itself. In Sweden, the mentor's partner is often called an adept. Protégé is old fashioned, with an air of patronage unsuitable in most organizations today. Mentee perhaps postulates a too one-sided relationship, all from the mentor, when we know that the relationship is two way. Mentoree seems the 'best of a bad bunch' and one which will be used here. The message is pragmatic—if you like it, use it; if not, use something else!

THE MENTORING SCHEME COORDINATOR

The role of the coordinator of the mentoring programme is to keep the aim and objectives of the scheme in the foreground for both the organization and participants. The coordinator should have a sound knowledge of the organization and excellent interpersonal skills. Part of their function will be to avoid problems arising in the mentor/mentoree relationship and, if they do occur, being swift and sure in diffusing the situation. If this is not done, the reputation of the initiative could be jeopardized. Monitoring of the relationship should be discreet, as an overactive interest precludes the privacy necessary for the mentoring relationship to prosper.

In rare circumstances, the coordinator may become a giver of feedback to both parties to the relationship. This may be a challenging situation if the mentor is a very senior person in the organization. Part of the process of giving feedback may lead the coordinator into the realm of coaching inexperienced mentors in their role. Coordinators need a thorough understanding of mentoring and should evaluate the organizational benefits of mentoring as the initiative progresses.

THE MENTORING CONTRACT

The essence of successful mentoring in an organizational context is managing the expectations of all the parties involved. For success, the organization should run a development event for the mentors and mentorees (separately) and ideally also for the line managers of the mentorees. This 'training' should not concentrate on the skills of mentoring, which is a different issue, but on the dynamics of mentoring itself.

From research I have developed a model called the Mentoring Contract that effectively manages those expectations as well as assisting the organization in avoiding the 'black holes' of implementation. The main headings of the Mentoring Contract are:

- A 'no fault' opt-out clause
- A two-way process
- What we are prepared to do/talk about
- Each other's expectations
- Time issues
- How much
- When
- In worktime/place or not
- Managing the line manager relationship
- Handling feedback
- Perceptions and subtlety
- Coping with envy/gossip
- Confidentiality of the relationship—trust/confidence
- Networking opportunities
- Learning about other aspects of the organization
- Life after 'the end'.

The contract is not written down, though it could be. However, it forms the basis of a dialogue between the mentor and the mentoree at the start of their mentoring relationship. We shall look at each part of the contract in more detail later.

REASONS FOR MENTORING

As discussed in Chapter 1, mentoring is not a panacea for all management development ills. It is a powerful strategic organizational development strategy, which if used properly can assist change in organizations. It remains a useful management development tool when it has a positive impact on the lives of individuals in organizations. However, mentoring for its own sake should not be attempted. Mentoring must have a valid and identifiable business case to be successful.

To some extent the way that mentoring is implemented in an organization will depend on the business case. For example, the way that mentoring would be organized for high-potential senior managers would be different in some of its dynamics from the way that mentoring would be implemented for new graduate recruits. That said, there are many features of mentoring that will be relevant to different types of mentoring scheme. So what kinds of issues and processes are pertinent for organizations which are thinking of using mentoring?

As organizations flatten and become more responsive to their markets, away from traditional 'silo' structures, senior managers are often brought into more frequent contact with people further down the organization. This enables them to become a resource in a very direct way to people involved in the 'sharper end' of the business. We have research evidence that mentoring can help to improve leadership styles in *mentors* as much as mentorees, which in turn can foster teamwork and cooperation in the business.

Zaleznik, in a seminal article in the Harvard Business Review (1992), has distinguished leaders from managers. He sees 'development through personal mastery which impels an individual to struggle for psychological and social change'. He goes on to say that for organizations to seek the development of leaders as opposed to managers, they would need to encourage one-to-one relationships between junior and senior levels of management, while at the same time nurturing individualism. 'Mentors take risks with people . . . the risks do not always appear to pay off but the willingness to take them appears crucial in developing leaders.' This is evidenced by TSB Bank which has used mentoring to build leadership rather than management in its businesses.

KEY ISSUES FOR MENTORING AND THE ORGANIZATION

Organization

- Mentoring can be formalized in the organization.
- A well-designed mentoring programme can help to develop competitive edge.
- Mentoring is not exclusive to one type of organization or sector.
- Replicated individual management behaviour becomes organizational behaviour.
- The culture of the organization will be crucial to the successful implementation of the mentoring programme.

Change

- Mentoring can assist in the leadership of change.

Leadership

- Development of leadership has been a traditional reason for mentoring relationships in organizations.
- The willingness of mentors to take risks with people is crucial in developing leaders.
- The development of new leadership styles can be encouraged by the mentoring relationship.

Individuals

- Senior managers need to become aware of their potential role as mentors.
- A powerful relationship exists between mentoring and developing creative insights.
- Mentoring can assist in the transition from middle to senior management.
- Mentoring can enhance individual and organizational learning.
- Mentoring can help alleviate the stress caused by major organizational change.
- Mentoring relationships can enhance communication within increasingly diverse workforces.

SOME KEY THOUGHTS BEFORE IMPLEMENTING MENTORING

- What are your real requirements for a mentoring programme?
- Can a mentoring programme achieve them?
- Can your organizational culture support a mentoring initiative?
- Are top leaders committed?
- Only volunteers will be useful in a mentoring programme.
- The role of the HR function as organizer of the mentoring programme.

- Should the process be managed by a dedicated internal or external consultant?
- Communicate the aims of the programme to all.
- Mentors need time and usually reasonable geographical proximity to their mentorees.
- Women and minority groups especially can benefit from mentoring.
- There is no single mentoring personality profile—all mentors do it differently.

POTENTIAL CHALLENGES TO MENTORING

Before introducing a mentoring programme into an organization, it is prudent to consider potential problems that may arise. Thinking about in advance and signalling them to the mentors and mentorees may assist in preventing them.

The Mentor

Bensahel says that it is possible for the mentoree (the word protégé is used) to feel suffocated by the mentor's influence. Strategies recommended for dealing with this include:

- The mentor not assuming that the relationship that they have developed successfully previously will work equally well for the mentoree.
- Ensuring that the mentoree is not 'dazzled' by the mentor's influence, by each noticing the balance of the conversations or if the mentoree is acquiring the habits, traits or quirks of the mentor.
- By not trying too hard to shield the mentoree from mistakes that are bound to happen through inexperience and also by avoiding confining the mentoree's growth potential to the limitations of the mentor.

Zey (1984) highlights several other possible problems for mentors in the relationship. They are:

- A lack of time/energy. Mentors expend time and energy on the mentoree (again the word protégé is used) that could be spent on the business.

- The risk of self-exposure. Mentors shed protective psychic layers in discussing their own weaknesses and failures with the mentoree. Mentors commit emotionally to the mentoree.
- The risk to their reputation. The mentoree with whom a mentor is identified may reflect poorly on the mentor, alienating key managers.
- The risk of having an incompetent mentoree. The mentoree can injure the mentor's organizational position by performing poorly in the job after a mentor influences their promotion into it.
- The mentoree's resignation. Mentors lose influence or position because their judgement in allocating time and resources to a mentoree who subsequently leaves the firm may result in adverse criticism and/or a decline in influence or power.

The Mentoree

For the mentoree, the risks are just as great. Zey highlights specific concerns that the potential mentoree should bear in mind in selecting a mentor:

- Is the mentor good at what he/she does?
- Is the mentor getting support?
- How does the organization judge the mentor?
- Is the mentor a good teacher?
- Is the mentor a good motivator?
- What are the mentoree's needs and goals?
- What are the needs and goals of the prospective mentor?
- How powerful is the mentor?
- Is the mentor secure in his/her own position?

Just as the mentor can be adversely affected by an incompetent or disloyal mentoree, the mentoree can suffer by being too closely identified with a mentor who is clearly losing power and influence in the organization.

Trouble spots in the relationship can be avoided or ameliorated by observing warning signs such as:

- the mentor suffering a career setback
- changing interests on the part of either mentor or mentoree
- differences in judgement between the mentor and mentoree

- undue involvement in personal problems
- changing business environments for either party.

One area of difficulty may be the ending of the relationship. Because of the inherent commitment, it is possible for the ending to be at worst traumatic or unsatisfactory. The mentor and mentoree must be fully aware of the potential for feelings of loss or dissatisfaction if the relationship is ended prematurely. This potential problem may be mitigated to some extent by the programme coordinator talking through the expectation for the end from the inception of the programme.

A CHECKLIST FOR IMPLEMENTING MENTORING SUCCESSFULLY

Before

- Why do you need a mentoring programme or some other paired support relationship?
- What are your aims for the programme? Check if mentoring is happening already.
- Is mentoring consonant with your organizational values?
- Who will be involved? Who will run the programme?
- What problems do you anticipate?

Mentor Profile

- Look for experienced, well-rounded senior individuals to be mentors.
- Find potential mentors who are people oriented and interested in the development of others.
- Mentoring is not age specific—experience is more important than age in being a mentor. Encourage qualified, younger managers to become mentors to prove it.
- Provide appropriate training for participants.

Mentoree Profile

- Decide who will be mentorees and why. What is your aim for this group?

- Choose acceptable and valuable mentorees for the programme. This may involve preparing a profile of your ideal mentoree.
- Be aware that the choice of mentorees can have political implications for the mentors' careers.

Who Coordinates the Mentoring Programme?

- The coordinator is usually a senior HR manager.
- Persuade a member of top management to have overall responsibility for the programme.
- Make senior managers aware of their role as mentors.
- Coordinators must have a sound knowledge of the organization.
- Coordinators will need the skills and personality to prevent/alleviate problems.
- Coordinators should be responsible for the final choice of suitable participants in the scheme, evaluating the scheme on an ongoing basis and being its protector.

How to Achieve Successful Mentoring

- Use volunteer participants in a pilot scheme.
- State the involvement and support of top management.
- Link the mentoring programme to other development effort.
- Keep the programme stage short and build in flexibility.
- Organize a Mentoring Contract for your organization.
- Make all participants aware of the potential risks, problems and benefits.
- Orient mentors, mentorees and line managers before the programme begins.
- Have a developmental diagnosis for each mentoree.
- Provide support for mentors and mentorees.
- Screen each mentor and mentoree.
- Monitor discreetly.
- Implement an effective evaluation system linked to the objectives of the mentoring scheme.
- Ensure confidentiality in the systems of the programme.
- Ensure that mentors have sufficient time for and proximity to mentorees.
- Have a time limit for the duration of the mentoring programme.

After

- At the conclusion of the programme, encourage top management to evaluate its success in meeting its objectives.
- Evaluate the programme during its progress and ensure that top management stays in touch with the process and is seen to do so, by becoming mentors themselves.
- Debrief and obtain feedback, using an external source, to obtain an overall picture of the initiative.
- Ensure that the learning associated with the programme is widely shared in the organization to allow continuous improvement to occur.

MENTORING AND THE ORGANIZATION—THE FUTURE

The complexity of the issues and nature of the challenges now facing many organizations mean that individuals need to adapt quickly and develop new competencies. Paired support relationships like mentoring can, when linked to key strategic organizational goals, lead to greater success.

Highly radical changes have occurred such as the change from national economies to a global economy and from hierarchies to networking. Percy Barnevik, chief executive of ABB (a Swedish-Swiss international company that has used mentoring successfully for many years), has exhorted us to 'think global; act local'. People in organizations need help to face these challenges and the mentoring process can contribute to this. Murray and Owen (1991) talk about changing the typically reactive behaviour of US business leaders and the part that mentoring can play in this process.

Mentoring can assist in facing some quite specific organizational challenges. As organizations change and flatten to form matrices, gaps can form in traditional relationships and reporting structures. A lack of personal or professional expertise or motivation may not be so apparent with the demise of these traditional structures. Mentoring can provide support for people working more in isolation than before. A recent example from the IT industry illustrates this. The organizational way of working involves project management in a series of several, relatively short-term assignments, reporting to several line managers. Because of this mobility and diluted authority, it becomes difficult for these line managers actively to support an individual's career development. The proposed solution was to appoint mentors to assist individuals in plotting their career development.

The use of mentoring not just for leadership succession purposes but as a means of developing all employees will diminish the credibility of charges of élitism and exclusivity. There is a new awareness that managers today are responsible for their own learning. Self-managed development is an approach that seeks to implement this concept. In management self-development the teacher is assigned the role of facilitator—a helper or enabler rather than an initiator. Teachers and trainers can help learners choose goals, resources and methods for learning, but they can no longer assume that they know best in defining another's needs or directly teach what they need to know. Many self-development designs use tasks or action learning as vehicles. A mentor's role can fit well with this approach and form a bridge between the individual's learning and the learning of the organization.

New discoveries can be replicated throughout an organization by a caucus of powerful mentors. Learning organizations often develop in response to powerful external stimuli, such as fast-moving change. A mentoring programme can keep pace with change and help unleash individual potential and talent, assisting in creating the learning organization. This, in turn, enables the organization to achieve a competitive edge, to survive and to prosper.

Chapter 4

Mentoring and Training and Development

One of the key decisions is the training and development options and approaches to be adopted when introducing mentoring into an organization. There are no unilateral solutions and a highly tailored approach is necessary for success. This chapter offers some general advice that may be of use to management developers.

As we have seen, there are two strands to the implementation of mentoring. The first is the strategic organizational development approach which involves building the business case for mentoring—taking a broad view of who will be involved, how it is envisaged that the scheme will be designed and will operate and its evaluation. The second looks at the impact of the initiative on individuals and their development.

Mentoring is a relationship, not a process, so any training and development scenarios have to take account of this. Anything that smacks too much of a process that is inflicted on the participants will receive a cool reception. There are various approaches—just choose the right one for you.

SENIOR MANAGEMENT AS MENTORS

Chief executives, board members and senior management generally are 'training shy', particularly in an area such as mentoring, where people feel that they have a natural aptitude and ability to perform successfully. This group is going to be the most difficult to convince that they should spend some time, however short, on becoming a good mentor. Successfully gaining involvement and commitment from these levels of management must include presenting any 'training' as a briefing (information giving) and facilitation (an opportunity to ask questions and impart confidence in the approach). This group has to be in control and if they feel that this is the case, there will be greater levels of comfort all around.

There are several situations in which you may find yourself (particularly as a consultant). One of the worst-case scenarios is that you have the task of briefing the board on the concept of mentoring, getting approval for the mentoring initiative *and* trying to give them some pointers on performing the role of mentor. This is not an approach to be recommended. A better situation is when approval and commitment have been obtained for the mentoring initiative prior to meeting the board. The mentors' development event should ideally stand alone and not be part of another development event or tagged on to a board meeting, as people may receive mixed messages, there will be time pressures and they may well be less receptive due to sheer fatigue.

The important thing to do is to manage the participants' expectations. It is good organizational practice, particularly at this level, to remember not to assume anything on the part of the participants. It is unlikely that any briefing documents have been read, so there will be a need to give context to the initiative. It is also important to communicate that this initiative has already been agreed and that the purpose of the meeting is to brief them, not to get permission. I well remember being at a specially convened meeting of directors, billed as a development event about mentoring, which nearly deteriorated into a second debate about the pros and cons of using mentoring. Do not give any opponents of mentoring a second bite at the cherry!

While we should encourage mentors to network and seek mutual support and advice, the issue of confidentiality needs to be emphasized, particularly in relation to 'high flyer' schemes. Top managers need to remember that they should not be using mentoring as an informal organizational assessment tool.

MIDDLE AND JUNIOR MANAGEMENT AS MENTORS

It is easier to design something for people further down the management ladder, in that they are often still actively involved in training and development events and junior staff are still often building competencies. It may be appropriate to include some exercises in the development event. However, it is a mistake to combine skills training and your mentoring orientation event. If a person needs to improve skills in the areas of listening, questioning and interpersonal skills generally, these need to be dealt with as a separate individual development issue. Apart from development best practice, not all the potential mentors need or will appreciate a good 'sheep dipping'.

As one gets further down the organizational management hierarchy, it becomes necessary to emphasize that mentoring is a sophisticated approach and can be corrupted very easily. It is very important to reassure line managers and supervisors that traditional line structures and responsibilities are not being eroded and that mentoring is an additional, potentially beneficial approach to assist in the development of people at all levels. It becomes more important to select and encourage the best-equipped managers as mentors to ensure success and quicker, relatively easy wins. Then communicate and build on that success.

One of the 'secrets' of any development event is not to get into overkill and bore the life out of everyone. When some organizations hold development events for mentors and mentorees (alas, not many include any development for the line managers of mentorees), they spend two days on a mentor development programme. This *may* be reasonable for very junior staff, but is totally unrealistic for senior people, as is a one-day event. The prospect of a whole day on mentoring for senior management could derail the entire project. In reality, everything that needs to be aired can be done in a half-day session of about two to three hours. If people wish to continue discussions, a morning session can be organized with a light working lunch at the end. Avoid specific exercises or mentor practice sessions for top managers. If people need help, it should be done discreetly, on a one-to-one basis.

Below is an example of a not untypical event for mentors that has been used successfully. The timings are approximate and the format is tentative. It should be about top-class facilitation backed up by expert knowledge. You get the result if you have covered all the issues that need to be covered by the end. *Do not attempt to railroad the participants through this timetable.* The format looks simple but will require expert design and delivery, so do not be tempted to say that this is simple stuff and pass it on to a junior in-house trainer. The credibility and expertise of the facilitator form a crucial part of the process, particularly at senior level.

A Half-Day Event for Mentors

09.30	Introduction and aim of the mentoring scheme
09.45	What is mentoring? How is it different from coaching? Fit with leadership? Benchmarking mentoring—the 'blue chip' experience
10.15	Setting the mentoring contract, including scheme terms and guidelines:

Terms

- 'No fault' opt-out clause
- Time is important
- Review after 9–12 months
- Mentoring relationship as a privilege
- Existing process of the organization
- Confidentiality
- Matching

Guidelines

- Regular contact
- Two-way relationship
- Building trust
- Set own parameters

Other issues

- What prepared to do/talk about
- Understanding expectations
- What help is available—role of HR
- Feedback—style
- Issues of those without mentors

- Where—mentoring in/out of work?
- Networking—learning about other aspects of the organization
- Life after 'the end'

11.15	Group work Exercise A (i) Relationship with line manager (ii) Invoking the opt-out clause
11.30	Group work Exercise B (i) Confidentiality—mentor (ii) Confidentiality—mentoring partner
11.45	Mentor's expectations of the scheme and what your mentoring partner will want
12.15	Final discussion—questions
12.30	Close

This event attempts to build in the content of the mentoring contract in a sensible and user-friendly way. The relevant headings should be taken as a starting point for discussion of, for example, how frequently people might think of meeting at first. The content consists of the terms of mentoring that the organization wishes to see included in all mentoring relationships. This is not to build in uniformity, but to ensure that there are common structures and terms available to all participants. It is important, for example, that there is a uniform organizational approach to terminating unsuccessful mentoring relationships—the 'get-out clause' in our mentoring contract. This part relates to the organizational development issues but not exclusively so. Other elements provide guidance on important issues that need to be borne in mind by the participants in the mentoring relationships.

The question of whether or not to use exercises in an event of this type depends on several factors. One of these is the seniority of the group. It would be inappropriate to use exercises with a very senior group—unless there was unanimous demand from the participants. Even then, a better approach might be to talk them through the issues raised by the exercises. For the same reasons, it would be inappropriate in most cases at senior level to practise conducting the first mentoring interview. A more acceptable and successful approach is to raise awareness of the need to give structured thought to this on an individual basis, privately and outside of the event you are running.

DEVELOPING MENTOREES

One of the commonest errors that organizations make when initiating mentoring is to forget about managing the expectations of the partners of the mentors. Developing mentorees is a crucial factor in deciding how successful the mentoring initiative will become. It is of equal importance with developing mentors. Imagine that only the mentors in an organizational mentoring initiative attend a development event. That does two things at once—it puts the burden of explaining what is going on firmly on the mentors and inculcates an initial dependence on the mentor by the mentoree for information. We are trying to avoid any form of dependence. In addition, the mentorees have a right to be told by the organization the purpose of the mentoring scheme and their role and responsibilities. Lastly, it is a good organizational check that the right message is being conveyed as well as reinforcing the view that in the mentoring relationship people should be able to interact on a basis of equality, irrespective of their seniority in the organization itself.

Assuming that best practice is followed and some development for mentorees is envisaged, the design and delivery of the planned event must be consistent with the messages that should be given about the nature of mentoring itself. Hence, the events should be facilitated and directly responsive to the needs of the participants. It needs to be differentiated from a standard 'training' intervention. Once more, the skills of the leaders of the event will be very important to success.

The event should aim to achieve several different but complementary objectives. The first is to outline the organizational case for mentoring and discuss the *raison d'être* of the approach. The event needs to inform, clarify and provide an opportunity to discuss the working of the scheme as well the dynamics of the approach as it affects participants. Finally and just as importantly, the event should give participants the confidence and enhanced motivation to start a mentoring relationship. The organizational coordinator of the scheme (usually but not always someone from the HR function) should endeavour to persuade a member of senior management to say a few words at the start of the event to underline the commitment of top management to mentoring. Such an intervention may help to dispel any residual cynicism that may exist in some participants.

In terms of the format, the content of the event will resemble that for mentors—it is the emphasis and tailoring that will make it different.

Also, a good facilitator will be something of an honest broker between the mentors and the mentorees in their workshops, allaying fears and encouraging them by helping the communication process between the groups. For example, it is possible to reveal the expectations of the mentors as a group to the mentorees. This will be group to group and not revealing specific, individual concerns, of course.

LINE MANAGERS OF MENTOREES

This group hardly receives any attention at all during the development process. However, potentially it has the greatest power to derail the mentoring initiative at the organizational level and in some organizational cultures its members need reassurance more than do the mentors and the mentorees. Organizational mentoring relies on trios, not duos. This does not mean that line managers have to be directly involved in the mentoring relationships of their reports, but it does mean that they have to be comfortable with the concept and practice of mentoring. One of the worst scenarios for an organization is that mentoring is misused in such a way that it corrupts the line processes of management, development and discipline.

Some organizations go so far as to say that they will not encourage a mentoring initiative if there are major objections from line management. This may be taking things too far, but there is no doubt that there is a responsibility on the mentoring scheme coordinators to inform line managers about the mentoring scheme, its aims, operation and critical success factors. Line managers are naturally concerned that their responsibilities for the development of reports may be eroded and also that they themselves will be viewed negatively by the mentors. This is particularly true if the direct managers of mentorees' line managers are selected as mentors. It is no exaggeration to say that this must *never* happen when matching mentors and mentorees. One of the most effective methods of getting the line managers of mentorees on board and understanding the dynamics of mentoring is to encourage them to become mentors themselves.

MENTORING MESSAGES

One of the most important things that is necessary when introducing mentoring into an organization is transparency. Some organizations produce guides for mentors, a separate guide for mentorees and yet another for scheme managers. In terms of best practice, there is no hesitation in saying that everyone should have access to the same information. This has several advantages: it prevents different groups from thinking that there is a hidden agenda, it promotes openness and easier communication between the groups of participants and it is more convenient and cost effective for the organization. The raining and development events should reflect the message of mentoring —individuals drive their own learning.

DIAGNOSIS OF NEEDS

When introducing mentoring into an organization, we are faced with people at different levels of experience, perceptions of mentoring and receptivity to the concept. Accordingly, they will have different needs to be met by the development process. The development needs matrix in Figure 4.1 is perhaps a logical starting point for the participants in the mentoring initiative.

How this matrix is used will depend on whether one is adopting a specific organizational mentoring approach or a 'whole organization' approach. By specific we mean that there exists a discrete group of mentors and mentorees with a defined set of objectives for the mentoring initiative, for example a group of high-potential mentorees or graduates. The second type of approach involves an open invitation to all the people in an organization to become familiar with the concept of mentoring and to take it up. Obviously, the dynamics of these two approaches will be different and the development needs will also therefore be met differently.

Specific Organizational Mentoring

Where mentoring is being introduced into an organization, one of the first things to do is to try to find out if there are mentoring relationships already in existence that people would be happy to acknowledge. A small-scale qualitative study of these relationships will give valuable information about the best way to introduce a scheme. This methodology can also be used in the whole organization approach. An evaluation of what has been happening to these mentoring pairs

Diagnosis of Needs

Mentors	Needs and development strategy
Existing and positive	
Existing and negative	
Potential and positive	
Potential and negative	
Uncertain	
Mentorees	
Existing and positive	
Existing and negative	
Potential and positive	
Potential and negative	
Uncertain	
Line managers	
Existing mentoring relationship of direct report	
Existing and positive about mentoring	
Existing and negative about mentoring	
Uncertain about mentoring	
Unaware of any mentoring relationship	
Potential mentoring relationship of direct report	
Potential and positive about mentoring	
Potential and negative about mentoring	
Uncertain about mentoring	
Unaware of potential mentoring relationship	

Figure 4.1 Organizational Mentoring Needs Matrix

can give useful insights into such matters as how colleagues of the pairs reacted to the mentoring relationship, or even if they knew about it. This could be useful in providing information on the likely attitudes of line managers of mentorees. It will also give a good guide to the sort of scheme terms and conditions that the organization should apply in a tailored scheme. The evaluation will also highlight the concerns of both mentors and mentorees, which can help to win over cynical, negative or uncertain potential mentors and line managers.

It is always useful to ask existing mentors who are positive about their experiences to talk with potential mentors. This may occur on a private basis or the mentoring scheme managers can arrange an informal opportunity, possibly over lunch to allow this to happen. With specific mentoring schemes, the numbers involved tend to be smaller, which allows mentoring scheme managers to work through the organizational mentoring needs matrix on an individual basis. It may be particularly important to involve senior management in helping to persuade reluctant line managers that they have nothing to fear from their reports taking up a mentoring relationship. It is very much an educational task for everyone concerned with the mentoring initiative.

Whole Organizational Mentoring

This approach is very different from specific tailored mentoring initiatives. It is much more akin to a change programme being rolled out with varying degrees of emphasis from the organization. It is true to say that this approach is less successful where mentoring is presented with a great deal of brouhaha in a way that change programmes and customer service initiatives sometimes are. This is a shotgun approach that covers a great deal of area but often has little penetration and so is best avoided.

A more successful whole organization approach is to present information on the concept of mentoring widely and be demand driven. Small pockets of interest should be encouraged to thrive and there should be an attempt to allow mentoring to become embedded in the organization so it can achieve organic growth and momentum.

One of the important things to understand is the effect of the organizational grapevine—it is essential that the right messages about mentoring are available. The main strategy for combating negative perceptions on the grapevine is education and it is important to have a range of different tools on hand. It is wise to create a Web site on the company intranet and to have readable and credible information in company magazines and newsletters. There are also more imaginative media such as videos. If you have some good examples of mentoring relationships or if people want to talk about the benefits of mentoring past relationships, it may be possible to put together a 'talking heads' video on a cost-effective basis and make this generally available to the organization. Another use of technology may be to create an on-line site where people can indicate their willingness to be mentors and/or mentorees and where they can give a short biographical note stating what experience they can bring to any mentoring relationship. This can be accessed directly by interested parties and takes responsibility for matching people (which can be demanding and resource hungry when done on a larger scale) away from the organization itself. It also reinforces the message that people are responsible for their own development and should be encouraged to be proactive in its pursuit.

The important thing here is to be in a position to handle any demand that is generated from the organization for mentoring—failure to do so could result in disappointment and cynicism about the mentoring initiative. Using the organizational mentoring needs matrix may stimulate a comprehensive approach about how to meet the differing needs of people in the organization who are interested in or likely to be affected by the mentoring experience. An interesting example of mentoring being used across the whole organizational spectrum is given below.

Z COMPANY PLC

Z Company plc is a subsidiary of an overseas manufacturing company. It is the holding company for a group engaged in the manufacture and trading of metals and chemicals as well as being manufacturers of domestic products. Z's markets are worldwide and have won several trade awards for export and technology. The company employs over 8000 people in the UK.

Mentoring Schemes

The organization has several distinct mentoring schemes for the following groups:

- Graduates
- Young high-potential managers
- Senior managers
- Managers on an MBA programme

Graduates

There is some crossover between this group and the MBA group. There are 32 graduates who are part of this scheme at the time of writing. The company has followed a deliberate policy of linking very senior management with the graduate group. This flies in the face of the concept of not linking people where there is too much of an experience gap. The reasoning behind this is to facilitate induction and to enable top management to assess the potential of the graduate group informally and over time. Both the mentors and mentorees have found that the differential levels have benefited their relationships, which are conducted in a relaxed way. This has provided great personal support to graduates. There is no threat to either group and the senior rank of the mentors enables them to act in a truly objective way in advising the graduates and acting in the longer-term best interests of the organization. The induction process is speeded up because line managers know that top management are actively 'policing' the process. Senior people can not only open doors for the graduate mentorees but also help to provide role models in organizational terms.

The term of the mentoring relationship is about 18 months, though no particular time is specified in advance. It has been found that the relationships tend to peter out as the needs of the mentorees decrease and they become more involved in their jobs. Also, the mentors tend to distance themselves more and move on.

What makes very senior management find precious time for mentoring junior management? They are often people who have a strong desire to help younger people. In addition, there are distinct organizational reasons and advantages in their spending the time, particularly in the identification of potential high flyers and successfully inducting and retaining a valuable managerial resource.

Young High-Potential Managers

There are 10 high-potential (HP) managers involved in this scheme at the moment. These are managers under the age of 35 who have been identified as being capable of reaching the operating boards of divisions as directors within five years.

Why choose mentoring? The organization has found that mentoring is effective in developing and motivating young people in high-stress roles. For example, there are divisions of the business which can be tough mentally and physically, with continuous operations requiring shift working at all levels.

Often, these younger people are managing a more mature workforce and the introduction of mentoring has helped the HP managers to become broader thinkers and to get support in dealing with organizational life.

This scheme is the most 'formal' in Z's mentoring portfolio. Mentors are directors of the division, who are assisted in their task by the divisional management development team. In addition, there exists a small committee of senior management and management developers who monitor progress both for individuals and from the organizational perspective, in terms of career management and succession planning.

The scheme has been judged a success because it is small scale, tightly focused and linked (via the committee approach) into the heart of the senior levels of the management structure. People feel that they can influence events and the mentors can influence the mentees' careers. A potential problem with this type of approach is the issue of confidentiality between mentor and mentee. As this is a high-potential management initiative, there is inevitably an element of assessment in the process. Assessment should not be a direct function of a mentor. The company has attempted to circumvent this challenge by the use of the committee. However, it takes exceptional objectivity on the part of the mentors to respect the confidentiality of the relationship while at the same time serving the wider organizational purpose of the scheme.

Senior Management Scheme

This scheme is for people at managing director level. These would be directors of individual business enterprises and there are eight in total. It was intended to formalize informal networks and to provide a way of increasing awareness of the parts of the organization where this is a development need. In addition, it provides an objective mechanism for discussion of issues on a 'level playing field' at this senior level. The reasoning behind this initiative is prompted by the role of the managing directors, which can be isolated and inward looking. The scheme improves decision-making quality and the mentor is encouraged to be a critical, challenging friend in a supportive and totally confidential atmosphere when major decisions are being taken. The mentor is at the same or senior level, although seniority is not a major issue for these people.

The scheme is working successfully. Time is not an issue, as these people have more flexibility and opportunities to meet both formally and informally. The relationships that are going on are of very good quality and, given the nature of the relationships at this level, it has been found that too much supervision of the relationships or 'policing' can be counter-productive.

MBA Candidates

Mentoring has been identified as necessary as part of a tailored qualification (MBA) programme in association with a well-known university provider. The MBA is seen as a vehicle to establish the mentoring relationship across projects and across functions. There are 63 people in the organization in the MBA group. The mentors selected were older than their mentees, experienced and good at helping people to think in a broader way. There was also a desire on the part of senior management and developers to get individuals to see that work itself is an opportunity to learn, as opposed to the notion that development equals training.

For the most part, the mentors were not MBAs themselves and were aged between mid-thirties and early forties. The company believes that there is a need for more than one champion for mentoring and that they need to be spread around the business, particularly in a multi-site operation. There is also a need to work hard to get real commitment in the initial stages of a scheme. The organization found one way of generating that commitment was to involve the line managers early on rather than later in the process.

The MBA programme is a three/four-year process. The mentoring relationships are not given a finish date and they either just stop or continue informally after the end of the programme.

SUPPORTING MENTORING

When mentoring is introduced in an organizational context it has to be supported at every stage. What this means in practice is creating systems that work well and also giving people the advice, development and confidence to carry out their roles in mentoring.

Mentors

Information and guidance are needed on what the role of the mentor should be in the organizational context. This can be provided in several complementary ways. Individual briefings from mentoring scheme managers are time consuming but must always be an option. It may be useful to turn the group of mentors into a mutual support group which can meet periodically to discuss, without breaching confidentiality, any concerns or challenges that the mentors may have. This will probably increase the quality of the mentors overall, which may be an important consideration if the organization has a fairly junior and inexperienced group.

However, the disadvantage of this approach is that it can look a little like overkill and may demotivate a group of busy mentors who are under time pressures in any event. The obvious solution is to run a short development workshop on what mentoring is and deal directly with people's expectations and concerns. The mentors will as part of this process meet other mentors, and having done so have formed, albeit informally, a low-key network. It makes sense for the mentor group to be demand driven and not put too many things in place that increase demands on the mentors.

Mentorees

Depending on the group of mentorees and the purpose of mentoring in the organizational context, different approaches are necessary. A group of high flyers will have their network firmly in place, but a development event will strengthen that. In the case of newly recruited graduates, it may be necessary to have some discreet monitoring from the mentoring scheme managers to ensure that all is well. Having said this, many organizations have sophisticated graduate recruitment programmes that may well help to fulfil this monitoring function. Again, the message is not to 'over-engineer' the mentoring initiative.

Line Managers

This group is ignored at the organization's peril as they are part of the critical success factors for organizational mentoring. It may not be possible to run a workshop for this group. If this cannot be done, the line must feel that they know what is involved in mentoring and it is the primary responsibility of the mentoree to explain, without breaching confidentiality, what mentoring involves. As we have seen, themselves becoming mentors to others often reassures line managers and supervisors. When running a small-scale mentoring initiative, it becomes more feasible for mentoring scheme managers to anticipate and help to correct concerns from individuals in this group.

Mentoring and Interpersonal Skills Development

For reasons already discussed, it is never a good idea to run a workshop that strives to put over the message about mentoring and to address the skills development issues of participants. If the organization has a 'standard' interpersonal skills event in its repertoire, that may be useful. However, as part of the process of implementing mentoring and building confidence and motivation among mentors, it may pay dividends to create a short, half-day to full-day event, that concentrates on some of the key skills associated with mentoring relationships. This may be required where the organization is using less senior managers as mentors.

The kinds of skills usually associated with good mentoring are those found in good facilitation. Yet paradoxically, if a mentor attempts to facilitate mentoring meetings, that will corrupt the relationship. The mentoree will feel that the relationship is unequal and will resent being 'processed' or manipulated. The key quality is building trust and on that basis using the sound employment of skills such as active listening and giving feedback in a supportive way. Coaching skills are not particularly relevant, except in so far as the mentor may actively be taking a coaching role as part of the relationship.

Evaluation of Mentoring

Evaluation performs two strategically important tasks in the implementation of mentoring in the organizational context. The first is that the information obtained helps to provide ongoing 'steering' for the initiative. The second and maybe more important function is positive reinforcement. Evaluation should not be a terminal operation carried out half-heartedly at the end of a pilot. It is also not a highly scientific, quantitative survey that produces a meaningless table of results. The best kind of evaluation in mentoring is as continuous as possible. The approach should be qualitative and some well-structured questions posed to a sample of the participants are going to be more productive in most cases. Evaluation should be carried out by someone who is external to the organization and who will be able to ensure confidentiality and elicit more open and valuable responses.

The evaluation process should be an active part of implementation and should serve as a stimulus to mentoring pairs who are not meeting as frequently as they might. The start of evaluation should give enough time for mentoring participants to get started and be early enough to pick up any common problems that need addressing. A good time to start the evaluation process is eight to ten weeks into the initiative, with an intermediate follow-up about twelve weeks after this and a final evaluation at the end of nine to twelve months from the inception of the programme. About twelve months is a good duration for a pilot programme, as the longer the programme is scheduled to last, the less interest there is from potential mentors who fear a long-term commitment. Most people are happy to sign up for a twelve-month programme.

It may be possible with larger numbers to include a questionnaire as part of the evaluation process, and this can give an indication of the scale of the impact of the mentoring initiative. For some organizations, harder measures of evaluation may look inviting. As part of the evaluation process it is possible to employ a form of 360 degree feedback to ascertain what changes mentorees have undergone, particularly if the mentoring programme has a highly specific set of objectives. A less stringent though related approach is to interview the mentorees' line managers. This has the disadvantage of being very subjective. It is also possible to take performance as a mentor into account when assessing overall management performance.

It has to be said that there are three main disadvantages to these 'hard' forms of evaluation. The first is the element of 'big brother'—it is over-policing the mentoring relationships which are very individualistic in operation. Secondly, mentoring is about personal development and the best judges of how things are going are the participants to the mentoring relationships. The third disadvantage is cost and the law of diminishing returns—any extra information obtained is unlikely to be gathered cost effectively. Evaluation should be simple, effective and transparent. The information should not be kept secret and a digest of the evaluation should be made available as a matter of course to the mentoring participants.

SHADOWING

Some people may be tempted to use the technique of shadowing as part of the way the mentoring relationship is conducted. It is used far more widely and successfully in coaching situations and is usually more appropriate for junior staff. Shadowing relies on prolonged and intensive personal contact over time and it may be said that over-zealous use of shadowing could end a beautiful mentoring relationship.

MENTORS AND NETWORKING

Mentors, like many of us, often do not realize the full extent and power of their networks. However, a word of caution—there is a world of difference between passing on the power of a network and active sponsorship in the organization. There is nothing wrong with individuals recommending their mentorees to others in the organization and it is a benefit for mentorees to establish integrated and enhanced relationships across the organization. However, where a recommendation from a mentor is acted on and promotion follows, there is a danger that others view the situation as favouritism. This is why it is important that mentors are not seen directly as assessors of organizational performance.

The good news for mentorees is that there is nothing wrong with a mentor putting in a good word where appropriate and justified and helping the visibility of a talented mentoree. Mentoring does, given human nature, provide some opportunities for discreet talent spotting. This can also, of course, be in the best interests of the organization. This whole area is one that requires a sophisticated understanding of organizational politics and the perceptions of others, as well as a realistic understanding by the mentorees of the world of the possible—unrealistic expectations in this area can lead to problems. Building this point into the development of mentors and especially mentorees will ensure that expectations are managed and not disappointed.

PROFILES OF MENTORS AND MENTOREES

There is no profile of the successful mentor, as we have seen. This applies also to mentorees. However, there are some expectations of each other that mentors and their mentoring partners share across widely differing organizations. Realism, understanding of the limits of the relationship, enthusiasm and above all commitment are important. Organizations do not need to draw up an 'ideal' mentor and mentoree profile—cloning has never been popular. However, an open examination of the kind of qualities that may be needed is a good idea.

This can work in two ways. The first is the more mundane level, looking at the kind of qualities that make a good mentor or acceptable mentoree in your organization. The second involves looking at the kind of strategic competencies that are necessary now and those that are becoming more important for enhanced performance in the organization as it develops into the immediate future. Without stepping into the world of role modelling—and most people do not wish to have or be role models as such—mentors who have valuable competencies should be sought out first when the organization is introducing mentoring. Psychometric tests are also not only unnecessary but may convey the wrong message—after all, when we are introduced to people at work we make our own assessments and do not ask for their psychological profiles. In fact, many mentoring relationships work because the participants have very different learning and management styles as well as personalities and this often brings freshness and real learning for both parties.

MENTORING AND GEOGRAPHY

Mentoring is about preparation, particularly where distances and time differences are involved. In all mentoring meetings preparation is particularly important, in the early stage of the relationship. As time goes on, spontaneity takes over but we tend to look for a structure for our discussions—unless we are just good friends 'shooting the breeze'. However, in the organizational context, mentoring does not necessarily mean friendship. What is important when undertaking a mentoring relationship at a distance is that there is a form of preparation for the conversation. There must also be a commitment to its actually taking place.

The means of communication has to be appropriate. It is possible to discuss difficult or sensitive issues over the telephone, which may be the only option. It is certainly better than videoconferencing, which is probably excluded for most people in terms of cost. E-mail and computer-based contact are not personal and may be read by others, which can preclude a real exchange of views. Any converging travel arrangements tend to be utilized by people in long-distance mentoring relationships and a great deal of mentoring is done in airport lounges and hotels. If we look at this proactively, there may be a need to allocate travel budgets to enable mentoring to have a fair chance of success.

Chapter 5

Mentoring and Developing High Flyers

Where mentoring is used in the organizational context, this is frequently to develop high-potential employees. The development of these individuals is for several different but complementary reasons. Organizations put in place many different strategies to develop talent and mentoring is becoming valued as one of the most cost-effective ways of assisting the growth of these key people.

SUCCESSION PLANNING

One of the main strategic reasons for developing high performers is succession planning. Organizations need to be sure that the best people are in the right place at the right time to optimize their performance. Best practice in management succession ensures that at least two results are obtained. First, the company should have people in place who are capable and effective to combat the loss of existing members of the management cadre through natural wastage and the attrition of competitors. Secondly, the development opportunities of the posts offered to these individuals should be sufficiently interesting to keep them motivated and happy.

STAFF RETENTION

This leads to another reason for using mentoring—retention. Many organizations today are lean and fast moving with, some might say, a large element of their success dependent on a disproportionately small number of individuals. Retaining, motivating and rewarding these people has become a major task for top management and a significant focus for senior HR practitioners.

So, you may say, if you pay these people enough they should stay. Unfortunately, it does not appear to be that simple. One of the main concerns to people building a career is visibility and recognition for excellence. An unfortunate result of many of the changes in the 1980s and early 1990s means that people are working under greater pressure and in more isolation. Very often individuals find themselves locked into a 'silo' pairing with their direct boss, who may be taking credit for the report's performance or wishes to keep a good report who is doing a good job and, by omission or even overtly, holds up their career progression. This may be in the interests of the boss, but it is counter-productive for the organization as a whole because it may now have a demotivated and less loyal employee who could be doing a 'bigger' job. A mentor can break this 'silo' and perform a role beneficial not just to the individual concerned but to the organization as a whole. Some individuals have been grateful for this 'safety valve' function of the mentor, who can often help them to retain a sense of motivation in difficult circumstances.

Of course, there are issues of confidentiality and interference in this scenario which need careful handling by the mentor. Mentors also have a subsidiary but important role in alleviating stress in their mentoring partners. While eschewing a strict counselling role, many mentors assist in diffusing difficult situations just by their normal activities. This benefit should not be under-valued.

BUILDING PERFORMANCE

Another benefit of mentoring at this level is that when we are discussing improving competencies, we are dealing with areas which often can be difficult to define and grasp. These are *performance* competencies, not threshold. That is to say, they are not so much about developing job capability but more about maximizing impact and playing in a higher league. Many organizations find it difficult to define the 'star quality' that they are looking for—but they 'know it when they see it'. Often the way to develop these more ephemeral competencies is not through formal learning programmes but in one-to-one learning dialogues with mentors. This approach is particularly well suited to senior cadre development and ensures that an organization can retain and enhance its competitive edge.

BUSINESS DEVELOPMENT

Evidence suggests that business development can be enhanced by using mentoring at this level in the organization. One of the advantages of pairing high-potential employees and high achievers with top management is that it can result in some very real bottom-line contributions, by giving people with new ideas access to top decision makers and cutting out time-wasting internal processes that can prevent new products and services getting to the marketplace before the competition.

NETWORKS AND COMMUNICATION

One leading global company has described its future as becoming a system of networks and processes. Barham and Oates, in their book *The International Manager* (1991) refer to the transnational corporation having:

> the following unique characteristics: an *integrated, networking structure*. International business now demands that every part of an organization collaborates, shares information, solves problems and collectively implements strategy. An integrated network is needed to share decision-making and enable components, products, resources and information and people to flow freely between the transnational's interdependent units.

The authors go on to describe a second characteristic:

> *Co-option*—A major problem in any world-wide business is that managers in key positions are often limited by narrow perspectives and parochial interests, leading to substandard decision-making. In particularly complex, multi-tiered organizations, this problem is often exacerbated by conflicting interests and overlapping responsibilities. The commitment of every individual employee has to be won to the overall corporate agenda, a process which the authors call 'co-option'. To develop such a consensus, each individual must understand, share and 'internalise' the company's purpose, values and key strategies.

The third characteristic, is the *co-ordination* of operations, and the related concept of socialization is described as 'a common corporate culture and a shared perspective among its managers'. Lastly, the authors mention the importance of innovation and its enablement: 'its ability to facilitate organizational learning by fostering a flow of intelligence, ideas and knowledge around the organization'. To create the transnational organization depends not on 'formal structures and reporting relationships—of much more importance is the need to change the attitudes and perceptions of managers and employees'.

This trend towards the transnational organization has implications for the development of the management cadre. These kind of issues are familiar change-management issues. However, one of the main problems of change management is sustaining the change. Positive and regular reinforcement of acceptable behaviours and mindsets is possible using the dialogue offered by the mentoring relationship. Many high-potential people have difficulty making the necessary adjustments required by operating at a global level or in a matrix structure. In such situations an experienced mentor can be an invaluable asset in saving time and trouble and achieving a higher level of performance. The mentor's network can play a significant part in giving assistance to high-potential managers in this type of situation. Also, as people progress in organizations they acquire additional mentor figures, sequentially or consecutively. These people can form a new set of valuable contacts and supporters within the corporate environment.

TALENT SPOTTING

This is a perfectly legitimate corporate aim for mentoring. Bright and capable individuals may be promoted to positions suitable to their talents. One advantage of a top manager as a mentor is that this person may be aware of up-coming opportunities before they are known to the rest of the organization. This, of course, is perceived as an advantage by the mentor's partner in the relationship.

It can also work in a more 'remedial' way. It may be that an individual is performing poorly in a particular role but the mentor has a high opinion of their potential. This may not be shared by others in the organization, for example the individual's immediate manager. However, the mentor may be able to arrange for the transfer of the poorly performing manager to another role where they may actually become a success. Without the input of the mentor it is possible for the organization to lose a capable employee who may well have been expensively recruited and developed. It is in this kind of situation where a mentor can work well within the framework of a cogent competency structure which allows an organization to make objective decisions about its people without resorting to more subjective methods of assessment.

MENTORS AND CAREER DEVELOPMENT

Mentoring can be a strategic approach to interest line management in career development issues. Generally, the more direct experience that senior managers have of the problems and opportunities surrounding career development in the organization, the better their understanding. Managers at all levels have to *believe* that the primary responsibility for developing people in the organization rests with them and not the HR function. In many organizations this is still an uphill struggle.

While interesting themselves in the career development of their mentoring partner, mentors themselves should not take on direct responsibility for that career development. This can require great self-control for some mentors, particularly if they are senior managers or they feel that the mentoring partner is receiving a raw deal from their line manager. Getting angry or frustrated on behalf of mentorees should not result in confrontation with their line managers. Mentors act in the mentorees' best interests when they act objectively and help them reach rational decisions.

Line managers and individuals share direct responsibility for career development, but mentors can be a powerful influence in helping the process. While not undermining the position of the line manager, the presence of the mentor can be a spur to the mentoree's manager to act correctly in career development matters. Most high flyers actively dislike any direct discussion between their line managers and their mentors and mentors should be advised accordingly.

BMG ENTERTAINMENT UK

Many different organizations use mentoring to develop high-potential people. However, to illustrate excellence in implementing mentoring for high-potential managers in a lean, creative, entrepreneurial and very fast-moving organization within an extremely competitive and challenging environment, BMG Entertainment offers many valuable insights. Mentoring has been designed in the company to assist the development of both individuals and the organization on many different levels.

BMG Entertainment UK is a highly sophisticated and successful component company of Bertelsmann AG. The company's business is diverse and broadly encompasses sourcing, marketing and distribution. In fact, the business is very much about rights. Famous names such as the RCA label come within its ambit and the company works with many well-known international recording artists. It employs 250 people at its UK headquarters in London.

Background

The culture at BMG is outwardly informal in many respects—not many suits and ties for internal consumption. But do not be taken in: this is a sharp and professional company. It does not like jargon and fights shy of many traditional 'training' approaches that are bread and butter to many other organizations. There is an open and questioning culture with a high emphasis on individual responsibility but in an overall team context. No one gets automatic respect here. There is a cadre of talented and ambitious young managers who are personally marketable within a small but competitive and well-rewarded industry environment.

Lianne Hornsey, now vice-president, HR for Europe, then directing HR for the UK, decided that, given the culture of BMG, mentoring might be one of the most productive approaches in attempting to meet several strategic development challenges for the company.

A pilot mentoring programme was *decided on* with conviction, rather than merely approved by the BMG board. It was to be a development activity for a select group of high-performing individuals at up to two levels from board appointment. The board members themselves and some very senior managers agreed to take on the role of mentors. The aim and benefits of the pilot were:

- to underpin effectively the cadre's career development and BMG's succession planning;
- to improve assimilation, leadership and operating style by personal support for the selected managers;
- to provide guidance to potential top managers, through suitable role models, in decoding and understanding the culture and processes of the organization and industry, but especially providing greater cross-functional knowledge of BMG-wide issues;

- to develop the skills and confidence of all participants and improve individual performance;
- to assist the organization in retaining valuable key personnel by encouraging loyalty and commitment;
- to provide greater understanding of senior management decision making and strategic approaches.

The mentoring scheme was supported by the human resource function, which at all times acted objectively and confidentially to keep the organizational objectives of the initiative in participants' minds.

The high-potential managers (mentorees) consisted of a group of 12 individuals. These individuals were asked to consider volunteeering to participate in this pilot. They were identified as complying with this selection template:

- identified through succession planning as having future potential;
- mentoring being compatible with other training and development planned with them for the immediate future.

The individuals to be mentors were in top management positions with sufficient experience and motivation to perform the role. They agreed to spend a half-day attending a development event to explore their role as mentors.

Mentoring had not been introduced within the company previously, so the mentoring initiative at BMG involved starting from 'cold'. This meant that the proposed process had to take account of the design and mechanics of the scheme itself, as well as training and developing the mentoring pilot participants. The design had to dovetail with other organizational and management development issues which were live, or became so, as the initiative progressed.

Implementation—the process

The process was divided into four stages.

The first stage involved identifying the type of approach and the processes that would be appropriate to establish mentoring within BMG. The main structures and outlines of introducing mentoring included the required profile of the mentor, preparing for the matching process, time constraints, duration of the mentoring relationships, challenges to the process, managing the scheme, correcting mismatches, getting support for the scheme and evaluation. After this stage was completed the design and mechanics of the scheme became evident.

The second stage involved the design and delivery of a half-day workshop for mentors. It covered the organizational issues of mentoring. A second half-day workshop was designed and delivered for the mentorees. The half-day workshops ran separately and provided the opportunity to tackle in a controlled environment the main issues that the mentors and their mentoring partners faced in the mentoring relationship. To achieve this, the workshops used the Mentoring Contract as a template. The approach was based on learning rather than training and enabled participants to manage their own post-event strategies in a supported way.

The next stage involved the design and implementation of the matching process for mentors and their mentoring partners based on the succession plan and the development needs, both current and future, of the high-potential managers selected for the mentoring pilot.

The last stage was setting a time to review the progress of the mentoring initiative and to provide a formal opportunity of monitoring the scheme and its impact to date and to incorporate significant learning for the future. This was done as one evaluation. Evaluation of mentoring is an *essential* part of the implementation process, since if it is done at just the right time it can provide positive reinforcement for the initiative—in other words it can 'jolly up' any backsliders!

In terms of evaluation, it is a good idea to source this externally in order to allow freedom of expression from the participants. Often, the evaluation can valuably highlight concerns that are not directly within the ambit of the evaluation. The BMG mentoring initiative was evaluated six months after inception. If thought useful, it was intended to cascade the mentoring concept to the next level of management, using the mentorees as mentors. The format and results of this evaluation report are reproduced here to give richness and depth to our view of mentoring best practice.

Evaluation Report on Mentoring at BMG Entertainment UK

Executive Summary

The role of mentoring has been seen by both mentors and mentorees as successful. The development that the mentors and mentorees have received has been judged to have been successful in managing the expectations of both parties to the mentoring relationship. There have been significant benefits to mentors and graduates and to BMG from the implementation of mentoring. In the light of this success, this report highlights specific recommendations and areas for further consideration and action as part of a process of continuous improvement of mentoring within BMG Entertainment.

Mentors
- Some mentors seek an input into the matching process.
- Mentors need to be proactive in their roles.
- Mentors may wish to have a positive relationship with the mentorees' line managers.
- Mentors need to be impartial 'champions' to whom their mentorees can turn.
- Mentors are important safety valves for mentorees—important in retention issues.
- Mentors should have a say in the best next-stage mentoring placements for their mentorees.
- Mentors must agree their 'agenda' with the mentoree as soon as possible.
- Level/seniority of mentors is important—needs careful consideration.
- Mentors must positively encourage networking/network growing.
- If mentors keep records, they must use care/discretion and ensure confidentiality.
- Mentors must be fully briefed on all aspects of the role of mentoring by HR.
- Mentors can act to assist in alleviating stress in mentorees.

General
- The use of mentorees as mentors should be considered.
- The 'no fault opt-out' should be retained, though there were some reservations about using it by mentorees. They felt they could be seen as failures for using it.
- Line managers need more understanding of what is involved in the mentoring relationship if the mentoring scheme is extended.
- Networking is perceived to need further encouragement from management.
- Regular contact between the mentors and mentorees must happen. The less successful relationships had less contact. The reasons were lack of motivation from some mentors and mentorees and lack of time/opportunity.
- When organizations take responsibility for matching mentors and mentorees, early communication of that match to both is desirable.
- Both parties felt it is important to get real 'buy in' from mentors by spending time building the relationship early on.
- Some first meetings between mentors and mentorees were perceived as being too artificial. Where there was an immediate work issue or connection, that gave an immediate focus for useful discussions. This point has importance for future matching practice.
- The career development role of the mentor is prized by mentorees.

Main benefits to the mentorees
- Confidence building.
- Impartial advice.
- Gives access to top management to discuss ideas.
- Improves business development opportunities.
- Better strategic organizational understanding.
- Future career development advice.
- Ongoing personal support which helps clarify role and improves operational function and potential conflict management.

Benefits to mentors
- Clearer view of impact of BMG organizational management style.
- Better understanding of some organizational issues.
- Improved awareness of management style for some mentors.
- Opportunity to stop and reflect on the business.
- Opportunity to see the world through different eyes.
- Being challenged on perceived wisdom.

Introduction and background

The mentoring scheme operates as an important constituent part of the development of the senior cadre of BMG. Mentoring was introduced as a pilot for a selected group of senior managers with recognized potential in the Spring of 1996. This evaluation is taking place to review the impact of the mentoring initiative and to highlight learning which will be important both for the present initiative and the future. The key findings are contained in the Executive Summary and the major areas of interest are now discussed in more detail in the main body of this review.

Objectives of mentoring

The main organizational purposes for introducing mentoring in BMG Entertainment are to:
- underpin effectively mentorees' career development and BMG's succession planning;
- improve assimilation, leadership and operating style by personal support for mentorees;
- provide greater cross-functional knowledge of BMG-wide issues;
- develop the skills and confidence of mentorees and improve individual performance;

- assist BMG in retaining valuable key personnel by encouraging loyalty and commitment;
- assist greater understanding of top management decision making and strategy.

Evaluation methodology

The approach has been a series of semi-structured interviews with the population of mentors and mentorees from across BMG. The interview format is intended to question common elements, but at the same time to allow interviewees an opportunity to raise their issues spontaneously. The interview structure covered the following areas:

1. What were your initial expectations on hearing about the mentoring initiative? Have these changed?
2. How was the introduction of the mentoring scheme handled? What changes, if any, would you suggest?
3. What problems did you encounter in the mentoring relationship?
4. What is your relationship like with your mentor/mentoree?
5. What kind of things do you talk about within the relationship?
6. How, if at all, has mentoring affected your relationships with other colleagues?
7. Have you kept your mentoring relationship absolutely confidential?
8. How often have you met or had contact with each other? Where?
9. What have been the benefits of mentoring for you?
10. What have been the benefits to your partner in the mentoring relationship?
11. What have been the benefits for BMG? Can you give specific examples?
12. If mentoring were to be extended to other parts of the organization, what are, for you, the three critical success factors in implementing/using mentoring?
13. Any other comments?

The Interviews

General view of scheme

Both mentors and mentorees expressed themselves in favour of using mentoring. No person expressed a view that mentoring was either unnecessary or positively disliked it. The mentorees as a group thought that mentoring is one of the core development processes for them. Some mentors had previous experience of being involved in mentoring, as mentors and mentorees. Most mentorees had no previous experience of mentoring.

Many mentorees found the influence of the mentors beneficial in addressing 'grey areas' that cropped up from time to time. They felt it was important to have 'someone to go to' to help with interpreting things and found positive help with this approach. Mentors were seen as providing help with questions such as 'What should my next career move be?' Or 'How do I go about best exploiting this business development opportunity?' They felt impartiality was a key characteristic of their mentors.

Some mentorees expressed the view that they did not know what to expect from their individual mentors, but were aware that it was up to them to contribute to setting the guidelines and parameters of their own mentoring relationships.

Mentors should spend time thinking about their mentorees and particularly not assume too much knowledge and understanding on their part on all occasions.

Many mentorees felt that the choice of mentor is crucial and that it may be an idea to involve the mentor and mentoree more in this matching process.

There appear to be few organizational sensitivities from line managers in this situation, though some managers were curious to know what was going on in the mentoring relationships. The whole area of geography was not an issue as both mentors and mentorees are in HO locations. This has lent itself to a more informal, 'drop-in' policy for contact. Mentors and mentorees who travel a great deal experienced time problems.

The 'opt-out clause' of the mentoring contract was felt to be useful, though some mentorees said that they would be loath to use it, mainly because they would rather try and work at the mentoring relationship and that they would not wish to be perceived as having 'failed'. In this circumstance, they appear to be prepared to live with a non-functioning mentoring relationship. This is not ideal for the individual or the organization and more emphasis may need to be placed on the validity of this part of the process for any extension of the initiative.

Mentors in general did not take on the problems of the mentorees and solve their problems by exerting their organizational authority. Their approach was much more facilitative and thereby met the requirements of the mentorees in the mature way one would expect, while at the same time not infringing the line relationships of the company.

Mentors were perceived as useful 'safety valves' and there were instances noted of mentors acting to alleviate real stress in the mentorees. Some mentorees expressed concern that very senior figures as mentors prohibited a full discussion of some issues, but others were delighted to have senior people 'batting for them'. This is mentioned here for the sake of completeness, however it is not my view that this is a widespread or a major concern for mentorees as a whole. However, good peer group support between the mentoree group will undoubtedly lead to better networking.

Mentors thought that a process that brought them together to discuss issues around mentoring generally, without breaching confidentiality, would be a good thing, though time/availability would be an issue. Confidentiality was a non-issue in the sample. No one reported any breach of confidentiality.

Process and matching of the mentoring scheme

The mentors felt that their development and preparation were good and that there were no major problems with the way that this part of the scheme was carried out. Both internal and external resources were used to launch the initiative. It is evident that the element of development is achieving its objectives in terms of results and quality. The same comments were made in relation to the development of the mentorees.

Both parties to the relationship made the point that they felt early matching was important. Some mentorees felt that they met their mentors a little late and mentors should realize that it is important to contact their graduates as a matter of priority. Both mentors and mentorees felt that they needed an input into the matching process.

Mentorees will need different levels of support, but everyone appreciates the need to kick off the mentoring relationship on a positive and warm footing. Many mentors expressed the view that the first meeting should be held away from the workplace in a more relaxed social environment. In terms of the number of meetings held, the normal distribution applies. Some met monthly, some bi-monthly, some in a very *ad hoc* way. The common factor was that both parties felt that they were available to talk at any time and that the frequency would be driven by the needs of the mentorees. Both mentors and mentorees need to think carefully about the structure of their first meeting. Many people said that they would continue to meet and talk after the 'official end' of the mentoring relationship.

Some mentorees expressed the view that their line managers were behaving in a mentor-like way with them and they found that this closeness and trust with the line manager did not obviate the need for a mentor. It became added value for the mentoree. Mentors in general have been used to 'bounce ideas off', to talk about the business at large, and for some, personal things too. One mentoree expressed the value of the mentor this way: 'With my line manager, and we get on well, I stop and think should I say this? There are sensitivities. With my mentor, I feel I can be more open. This person is not in charge of me or my career and I feel more able to talk openly about my views and needs.'

Benefits to mentorees

Many mentorees feel that they are more confident in their approach as a result of having a mentor. They feel more in control because they have more information and have had an opportunity to test ideas before implementation. They feel that there is a safety valve where they can get unbiased and valuable feedback based on real experience. The experience of the mentors in the business is thought by mentorees to be one of the main parts of the USP of mentors in the organization.

Impartiality of the mentors is another part of their USP. Mentorees are more confident in being open where they feel that the mentor is not being judgemental or taking a 'party line'. Some mentorees feel that the inclusion of people who may have a say in their immediate future can lead to less openness on both sides. However, there is a realism among the mentorees that these relationships are part and parcel of organizational life and they have developed the skills and maturity to cope with them.

Some mentorees expressed the view that given the pressures of business life, it is easy to get sucked into the job and to lose perspective. The mentors play an invaluable part in keeping the mentorees focused on their careers. The line managers, with their focus on the task, are often less readily equipped to do so.

Both mentors and mentorees agree that mentorees get a better picture of the organization and greater understanding of their own and others' roles from the mentoring relationship. Mentors give a commercial overview and often a non-functional view to complement the business unit view of events/developments. Mentors give more open guidance on some of the political aspects of everyday existence in an organization and give background information that may not be readily available elsewhere in the business. One mentoree said that the mentor gave feedback that seemed to be based in reality.

The influence of the mentor in the area of career development is thought to be supremely important by the mentorees. The experience of mentors gives them an ideal opportunity to advise on career development. Individual mentorees have experienced problems with managers and mentors have been useful in assisting in resolving those issues. They have also been proactive in many cases in advising mentorees of opportunities.

Benefits to mentors

While it is true to say that most benefit has been received by the mentorees in this mentoring initiative, the mentors individually and collectively have indicated that they have seen the process as two way and have benefited from their contact with the mentorees.

Mentors reported a clearer perspective on the organization. There was a view that the ultimate impact of the management style and the decisions of the organization could be seen more clearly by mentors. Another mentor has said: 'mentoring is good at keeping my eyes open'. Thus organizational communication has been improved among the group involved in the mentoring scheme.

The opportunity to reflect on the decisions and conduct of organizational life is noted by many mentors. Talking through issues with mentorees has often brought real benefits and mentors themselves have bounced ideas off mentorees, though not always necessarily very obviously. The mentorees do provide fresh eyes, as one of the mentors put it. This has proved useful to mentors.

Mentorees have challenged the mentors throughout the mentoring process to justify the ways of the organization and this has resulted positively in the mentors confirming their role as change agents.

Examples of responses from the interviews

1. What were your initial expectations on hearing about the mentoring initiative? Have these changed?
    - 'Maybe thought it would be more about coaching around specific objectives.'
    - 'Thought it would be good for my career development.'
    - 'Mentoring is not about sponsorship.'
    - 'Relaxed way of learning about the business.'
    - 'To get at the culture of other bits of the business.'
    - 'Opportunity to get to know someone at board level well.'
    - 'Concern that mentoring could cut across the line.'
    - 'Wanted the mentor to be a champion.'
    - 'Expected openness.'
    - 'To learn more about the business.'
    - 'No clear objective, so it is difficult to measure for success.'
2. How was the introduction of the mentoring scheme handled? What changes, if any, would you suggest?
    - 'Process was OK.'
    - 'Maybe a choice in matching.'
    - 'OK. The reaction from the mentorees has been good.'
    - 'Expectations were managed well.'
    - 'It was flexible.'
    - 'Mentors were not sure who was responsible for initial contact.'
    - 'Intro was important, it cannot be skipped.'
    - 'Initial suspicions disappeared.'

3. What problems did you encounter in the mentoring relationship?
   - 'No. Very good relationship.'
   - 'We only met once.'
   - 'A lunch re-arranged four times.'
   - 'Time. They have made time but not been around.'
   - 'Diary of the mentoree—Time—not around.'
   - 'No problems.'
   - 'Struggle to get together.'
4. What is your relationship like with your mentor/mentoree?
   - 'Very good.'
   - 'Very equal.'
   - 'Lots of icebreaking.'
   - 'Very approachable.'
   - 'Shares, takes time.'
   - 'Spontaneous and informal.'
5. What kind of things do you talk about within the relationship?
   - 'Looking at the competition.'
   - 'Personal stuff.'
   - 'My ideas for the department.'
   - 'How we are seen from the outside.'
   - 'Corporate things.'
   - 'Things not related directly to the job.'
   - 'Giving a wider view and different angles.'
   - 'Practical things.'
   - 'Career development needs.'
   - 'What does BMG want.'
   - 'Promotions.'
   - 'Core business understanding.'
   - 'Mentoree's development.'
   - 'Need for more challenge.'
   - 'Peer/boss relationships.'
   - 'Problems with my boss.'
   - 'The issues, not personalities.'
   - 'Talked with a view of better understanding my mentoring colleague.'
6. How, if at all, has mentoring affected your relationships with other colleagues?
   - 'Mentoring has a low profile in BMG.'
   - 'Not at all. It has been confidential.'
   - 'No effect on others.'
   - 'No. Do colleagues know about it?'
   - 'No impact.'
   - 'No. My mentoree's manager is aware but it is totally confidential.'
   - 'There have been two/three instances of envy/gossip.'

7. Have you kept your mentoring relationship absolutely confidential?
    - 'Totally.'
    - 'Yes. Totally confidential.'
8. How often have you met or had contact with each other? Where?
    - 'Once.'
    - 'Three times—lunch and the office.'
    - '*Ad hoc*.'
    - 'For lunch mainly.'
    - 'I drop in.'
    - 'Five times in the office and lunch.'
    - 'Three meetings.'
    - 'Regular contact over two months.'
    - 'Six to seven times.'
    - 'Two meetings.'
    - 'Once every three weeks, then it tailed off.'
    - 'I need to use my mentor more.'
9. What have been the benefits of mentoring for you?
    - 'No real benefits.'
    - 'Not really, not used it.'
    - 'Get to know a person's strengths and weaknesses, their interests and long-term plans.'
    - 'To learn from him sometimes.'
    - 'Having the relationship has helped communication.'
    - 'Support and compassion when needed.'
    - 'Been very two way.'
    - 'Better business understanding.'
    - 'Good internal contact.'
    - 'More confidence about the big picture.'
    - 'Help in dealing with a difficult boss.'
    - 'Given me more confidence.'
    - 'Helpful access to develop a new business opportunity.'
10. What have been the benefits to your partner in the mentoring relationship?
    - 'Better understanding of what I do.'
    - 'Don't know.'
    - 'Access.'
    - 'Good advice.'
    - 'Being a sounding board.'
    - 'Shared experiences—good and bad.'
    - 'Understanding a different part of the business.'
    - 'Different pressures operate here—knowing what they are.'
11. What have been the benefits for BMG? Can you give specific examples?
    - 'Opportunity to get view on a business development possibility from a senior manager where I do not usually have contact. This will be beneficial to the bottom line.'

- 'Better knowledge of each other and what we do.'
- 'More communication.'
- 'Developing and refining our management skills in a time-effective way.'
- 'Helping people to stay in the organization.'
- 'Better decision making.'

12. If mentoring were to be extended to other parts of the organization, what are, for you, the three critical success factors in implementing/using mentoring?
    - 'Picking the right mentorees.'
    - 'Ensuring confidentiality.'
    - 'Training everyone involved.'
    - 'Picking the right time for it.'
    - 'Ensuring time is available for it.'
    - 'Find a way to make it happen organically.'
    - 'Do not let people collude in a negative way.'
    - 'Manage expectations.'
    - 'Preparation and training.'
13. Any other comments?

Conclusion

The mentoring initiative at BMG is working and seen by the participants as a success. Both mentors and mentorees have put energy and enthusiasm into making the mentoring relationships work. They have all done it differently and in their own way. However, the work that HR has done in laying good foundations for the mentoring scheme has been a vital ingredient in its success.

Since the Evaluation

The report was well received by the board of BMG. There was a view that mentoring fitted perfectly as an approach with BMG's culture and that participants had been comfortable with the experiences involved in introducing and using mentoring. Success had in one case been measured by a substantial new business opportunity which had been triggered by a particularly successful mentoring relationship. Thus by different measures the initiative was judged to be successful. The evaluation was done early enough for changes and various 'tweakings' to be done at a relatively early stage and this has prevented problems further down the road. Monitoring is an on-going process within the organization and the cascading of mentoring to the next management level has been initiated and is in progress.

There is some important specific learning from the BMG experience of mentoring that can usefully be imparted when considering mentoring for high flyers.

Seniority of mentors   This can be a benefit but can inhibit some people. It is useful to consider this when suggesting matches.

Matching   Both mentors and mentorees will want an input and should be sounded out informally when matching up participants to the mentoring initiative. There is no 'scientific' way of matching people and 'gut feel' about matches is as valid as anything else.

Information   Keep people informed and brief them fully. No one likes surprises!

Getting started and keeping going   At this level particularly, mentorees need to be proactive in establishing and maintaining the mentoring relationships.

Time   This is the greatest challenge. When mentoring meetings are cancelled, both parties have a duty to the other to ensure that they are rescheduled right away.

Distance   This can be a distinct challenge, particularly in a global environment. Mentors and mentorees need to explore all their options. It is amazing how much mentoring goes on in airport lounges!

Growing mentors   Mentoring replicates itself. Mentorees become mentors to others. No one should see themselves as permanently cast in a particular role. Many people are both mentor and mentoree at the same time at this level.

Line managers   Relationships with line managers and other mentors need careful handling to avoid problems. At this level politics can become more of an issue in the organizational context. Organizations need to protect mentoring from being seen negatively because of this.

And finally. . .   The basic principles of organizational mentoring apply to all cases. However, with mentoring for high flyers there are some important dynamics that should not be ignored. The organizational level and sophistication of the participants mean that extra preparation and reflection before the implementation process begins pay dividends. You will need to have all the answers to all the questions before you communicate to senior management your idea of using mentoring in your organization.

Chapter 6

Mentoring and Building Diversity in Organizations

Diversity is one of the 'buzzwords' of the 1990s management repertoire to which some organizations pay lip service. Significantly, many more organizations have woken up to the fact that it is no longer possible or desirable to ignore the contribution to organizational success of women or, for that matter, employees from other cultures, gay men and women, people with different capabilities and other significant 'minorities'.

The development of women in management can be specifically enhanced by effective mentoring and it is in this area that most work has been done by agencies and organizations to promote these valuable relationships. While this is not the place to discuss in detail the development of women, it is true to say that despite notable successes in recent years, many women still find the 'glass ceiling' to top management promotion firmly in place. So how does mentoring fit with assisting women to develop in organizations?

The kind of mentoring that was going on in organizations prior to the last decade was, with honourable exceptions, likely to be an *ad hoc*, patronage model that was designed to produce a cloned copy of the kind of management that had always succeeded in that particular corporate environment. Without straying into any minefields, it should be recognized that opportunities for so-called minorities were limited by this. What is interesting is that mentoring itself was not held by many of the disadvantaged to be the problem, but rather the type of mentoring model that was being used. Effective mentoring can be one of the best tools for building diversity within organizations.

A great deal of credit should go to pioneering work done by the US public administration in the 1970s, where mentoring schemes to develop diversity were encouraged and funded—one of the first was in the US Department of Agriculture. This is not to say that mentoring has to be bound up inextricably with positive action. In fact, mentoring can be a valid alternative to using positive action programmes.

Opportunity 2000, a UK initiative in the area, recognized that mentoring can be a powerful tool. In October 1995, Ashridge (a founding member), together with Opportunity 2000, hosted a mentoring symposium which was attended by a number of member organizations that were interested in the use of mentoring in organizations and how it can be used to implement equal opportunities strategies. As one of the event organizers, I was pleased to find that over a quarter of the organizations represented at the symposium already had experience of using mentoring.

Not surprisingly perhaps, Scandinavia, and particularly Sweden, was active in the late 1980s in adopting mentoring to encourage development for women in organizations. For the Ruter Dam programme (which is not just about mentoring but management development generally), based in Stockholm, mentoring has been a complementary approach based on informal processes and networks. Senior management in Swedish blue-chip companies are encouraged to recommend women in mid-career with potential to reach the top to take part. Most of the mentors in the programme are male senior managers, but not usually from the same organization as the women. This is an interesting, if élitist, approach to mentoring.

The mentoring initiative at ABB Sweden is a refreshing example of mentoring as an approach for all—men and women, and all employees, if they want it, not just management. However, the mentoring approach did start off as a scheme intended for helping the development of women. The approach at ABB Sweden is an example of an initiative that, while intended as something to benefit women, had a flavour of a 'whole organization' approach to it. This often finds favour in mentoring initiatives generally in continental Europe.

ABB SWEDEN

Asea Brown Boveri was formed in 1988 through the merger of the Swedish Asea and the Swiss BBC Brown Boveri and has 200 000 employees. ABB

Group operates a sophisticated matrix structure and is a global electrical engineering company, whose business encompasses a wide range of products primarily related to the generation, transmission, distribution and efficient use of electricity. Further areas of activity include rail transportation systems, industrial drives, equipment for process automation, oil and gas handling and metallurgical processes. ABB is also in fields such as industrial robots, power lines, air pollution control and general contracting. The company provides financing, insurance, leasing, treasury services and portfolio management for ABB companies and external third-party clients.

Sweden is one of ABB Group's important home markets, with most of the group's business areas represented across the entire electrical power sector.

We visited ABB Sweden's head office at Vasteras, 120km west of Stockholm. This is the Asea company town and contains around half of ABB Sweden's 20 000+ employees. At Vasteras, we were given an insight into how a mentoring initiative can grow from a small scheme with a specific business case into a wider approach with the potential to encompass the whole organization.

The personnel policy for ABB Sweden stated in 1993 confirms that 'satisfied customers and motivated employees are of vital importance to ABB's long term competitiveness'. The statement continues: 'each employee shall: understand his/her role; have the necessary empowerment; take responsibility; develop his/her competence, knowledge, will and ability.'

Eight substatements follow which give an overall context for the mentoring initiative as it developed. They are stated as:

- Clearly defined goals for both the individual and the work team shall be the cornerstones of our activities.
- Respect for and confidence in the individual shall characterize our work environment. This must be safe and stimulating.
- The local unions shall be natural cooperation partners.
- Each manager at ABB shall continually develop his/her management skills and leadership so as to be able to assume full responsibility for employees.
- Planning discussions shall be held at least once a year with each individual employee.
- The goals of our learning organization are to achieve a continuous development of competence, internal mobility as well as different employee development routes and career opportunities.
- Good ethics, equal opportunities for everybody and an open and honest exchange of thoughts and ideas are the cornerstone of our actions.
- The implementation of the personnel policy is a strategic issue in which we must all participate.

ABB believes that its success depends on being able to recruit, retain and develop the best managers in their fields. Their key selection criteria are competence and professionalism, including leadership, people skills, functional and administrative skills. The ABB belief is that human resource development is a key task for each line manager. This is intended to help to recruit and promote from within the ABB Group.

ABB Sweden's Mentoring Programme

Vision

- To be a natural part of the ABB culture and thereby to create opportunities for continuous transfer of knowledge and experience.

Objective

- To improve the situation of all employees at ABB and increase effectively work satisfaction and motivation.
- To maintain and develop competence within ABB, minimize differences between generations and between white-collar and blue-collar workers.

History

The first programme started in 1991 with 100 mentorees called adepts. This was a women-only programme. The 1992/93 programme had 225 adepts who were once more exclusively women. The programme was then opened to men as well as women. The total number of adepts grew to 260, of which 11 were women and 149 men. In 1994/95 an additional 176 adepts joined the scheme—83 women and 93 men. By 1996, around 11% of the workforce had *voluntarily* become adepts. If one adds in the number of mentors, this represents a significant proportion of the entire workforce, not just management who are involved in mentoring.

Mentors and adepts

In the programme starting in 1995, half of the adepts were men and half women; 50% of the men and 40% of the women were between 32 and 41 years of age. Very few were over 51 years old. While 10% of adepts were male managers, there were no managers among the female adepts.

Of the mentor population, 70% were men and 60% women. Both male and female mentors were between 42 and 51 years of age. The second largest group of male mentors were over 51 years old and the second largest group of female mentors were between 32 and 41. Only one mentor, a woman, was under 31 years old. Among mentors, 12% were female managers and 58% male managers.

Expectations

These were as follows:

Adepts
- Personal development
- Increase confidence
- Understand how managers think
- Get to know another company
- Find new direction (in work)
- 'Sanity check' (bounce ideas).

Adepts thought that the 'ideal' mentor is:

- open and honest
- a keen listener
- active and committed.

Mentors
- Personal development
- Help another person to develop themselves
- Be supportive
- Get to know another company
- Get to know another person's situation
- 'Sanity checker'.

Mentors thought that the 'ideal' adept is:

- open and honest
- open to change
- purposeful
- curious, interested in learning.

Evaluation

Most people expressed satisfaction with what they obtained from the programme. What benefits did the mentoring programme give them?

Adepts
- Personal growth and development (55%)
- See other person's situation (53%)
- Wider perspective on life (49%)
- New friend (38%)
- Greater self-awareness (36%).

Mentors
- Understand others' situation (90%)
- New friend (51%)
- Personal growth and development (38%)
- More knowledge of ABB (37%)
- Wider perspective on life (36%).

Almost one-third of the adepts have met their mentor when the line manager was present and 64% of these adepts believe that this had a positive effect.

Continuation

Some 70% of the adepts and 67% of the mentors want to stay in touch. Half of the adepts would like to be mentors themselves and 78% of the mentors would be happy to be a mentor for a new adept.

Summary

The case of ABB Sweden shows how a purely voluntary programme can get 'under the skin' of the organization in a relatively short space of time. The mentoring initiative at the company works on several different but complementary levels. First, it helps women to develop themselves. Secondly, mentoring helps to integrate the organization. Lastly, it is a powerful agent for culture change in involving and motivating the whole workforce.

It also illustrates that potentially the best way to introduce mentoring across the organization is to use a voluntary, small-scale pilot that grows organically. The way to grow it may be to encourage openness about the concept and practice of mentoring, by the management of the organization giving 'permission' for something that may be seen as a radical departure in cultural terms and by broadcasting success that will encourage people to buy in. Employee demand-led mentoring is the mentoring that is likely to stick and succeed.

A more traditional and highly structured approach in the cause of equal opportunities is that adopted by Brent council in London.

LONDON BOROUGH OF BRENT

The London Borough of Brent is a local authority responsible to a population of 260 000 people living in north-west London. The authority currently has nearly 6000 employees. In 1990 a poll of the borough's residents found a low satisfaction level with the council and its services. Since then, the organization, under the leadership of the chief executive Charles Wood, has embarked on a programme of continuous improvement based on a total quality approach.

The Brent Total Quality Programme was launched in July 1991. It is guided by a clear mission (to be simply the best), three core values (quality, efficiency and customer first) and nine organizational objectives (strong and committed leadership, the client/contractor split, a belief in total quality, clear accountability, customer-led services, total ownership of change, simple direct communication, maximum devolution and strong staff development). A 1993 poll showed remarkable changes in performance, with almost every service area showing quantifiable evidence of improvement and success. Brent is now a front runner in the latest developments affecting local government.

Aim of the Scheme

The results of a post-reorganization audit carried out by the HR unit in July 1992 revealed that 11% of senior managers were women, despite women forming 65% of the workforce. Brent has tried to achieve a workforce that is more representative of the community that it serves. To help remedy this situation, the Opportunity 2000 Group devised a mentorship scheme that is open exclusively to women middle managers. The initial scheme was a pilot of 15 mentees. The Brent Opportunity 2000 success criterion is: 'by 1995 there will be a significantly higher percentage of women managers in post in principal officer grades than there are at the moment in 1992'.

The Brent Women Managers Mentorship Scheme is one of the strategies the council has adopted to meet its Opportunity 2000 objectives. The council felt that research and the practical experience of many organizations has shown that when men are encouraged to act as mentors to women on a formal basis, this can help to break down some of the barriers that exclude women from getting to the top and it can assist them to move onwards and upwards in their career development.

Target Group to Be Mentored

Mentees were female staff graded between PO1A and PO2C—middle management grades. An equal opportunities monitoring study in 1990 found that 8% of the male workforce was located in grades PO1A–C, compared to 1% for women, eight times as many men as women. A comparative grade and gender survey, council wide for 1992 and 1993 shows an increase in women in grades PO2A–D for 1993 over the previous year. This is also true of the higher special grades above principal level.

Mentees needed the support of their line manager to apply successfully to the scheme. They were selected according to two criteria: the potential to progress to senior managerial level and the degree to which a mentorship relationship would enhance career prospects.

Target Mentors

Mentors were sought from volunteer male staff graded between grades Special A and PO2C. There was no explicit selection process. By including women mentors, the scheme acknowledged the preference of some women to be mentored by females. Mentors received at least one day of training in mentoring skills before being considered for the scheme.

One of the key requirements for mentors was that they had to be experienced people in the organization in order to assist in filling experiential gaps among the women being mentored. Although mentors were not chosen by skills (this being more of a coaching approach), where it was obvious that experience in a field such as finance would be useful, a woman manager with a need to develop this area could be matched with a senior financial manager.

Brent's Definition of Mentoring

Mentorship is a process by which senior staff share the benefits of their knowledge and experience with others by giving guidance on career management, personal development and organizational knowhow. It has the objective of assisting the mentee with their work and career. Mentors provide advice and guidance to people in more junior positions in an organizational situation. This guidance is usually given by senior staff after careful consideration of the planned topic of discussion. Mentors may act in a variety of roles: adviser, role model, facilitator, ideas person, counsellor, confidant, motivator, critic and friend. Mentors may provide the following types of support:

- Guidance in how to acquire the necessary skills and knowledge to do a new job.
- Advice on dealing with any administrative or people problems.

- Provision of information on 'the way things are done around here'—the corporate culture, core values, organizational behaviours and preferred management styles.
- Coaching in specific skills such as leadership, communication and time management.
- Help in tackling projects by pointing mentees in the right direction, in terms of contacts.
- A figure with whom the mentee can discuss their work, aspirations and concerns.

The Scheme and Process

The scheme was operated by the Corporate Personnel Group of the Council. The Steering Group of the Opportunity 2000 initiative had a number of roles in relation to the scheme: to review the matching of mentors to mentees; to feedback a review of the scheme's operation to the Corporate Personnel Group; to ensure that operational difficulties within the scheme are remedied; and to participate in the development of scheme rules and selection of mentorship training packages. In addition, due to the emphasis within the scheme on male mentorship of female staff, the role of scheme adviser was created. The scheme advisers were female, graded at PO2C or above, and received training in mentoring. Some were mentors themselves. The role of the three advisers appointed was to counsel mentees over problems with the scheme, counsel mentors over difficulties in their mentoring role and also to feedback difficulties over scheme operation to the Opportunity 2000 Steering Group;

The target group was identified, concentrating on women who had potential for senior management and were already acting as change agents. The purpose was to give people with potential an extra push. A letter was sent to the mentees with details of the mentors who had volunteered. The details were written by the mentors themselves and varied from one line to a paragraph giving information about themselves that might assist mentees in making a choice.

Guidance was given by the Human Resources Unit on the criteria to which the mentees should adhere when choosing by whom they would prefer to be mentored. These were:

- Personal preference of the mentee.
- Organization level—the need for an appropriate gap in experience.
- Not too senior a manager mentoring too junior a mentee.
- Areas of skills in which the mentees may have been lacking.

The mentees completed an application form, supported by the line manager. The matching process was carried out by the HR Unit on the basis of the mentors' strengths, the mentees' needs and the HR Unit's knowledge of both. However, mentee preference was always the first consideration in matching. The mentor may have possessed a particular skill or functional area of interest, but in all cases the expressed needs of the mentee were paramount. One of the key lessons was not to 'waste' the experience of a senior mentor on too junior a match, because an understanding gap would exist which would mean that the practical use of the relationship would be lost.

One of the key organizational needs to be met was the experiential gap among the mentees. It was recognised that the mentors selected would need real experience and a complete understanding of the organizational culture. As part of the selection process the mentees went through a battery of instruments—OPQ, Learning Styles Inventory—and received feedback appropriately.

The mentors were given a day's training which was partially successful in orienting the mentors to their role. This is an area which proved to be one of the greatest challenges to those running the scheme. Identifying and flagging the issues and putting structure and process in place, while at the same time highlighting the skills, proved too difficult given the original design of the event. The mentors' day focused more on the process and, as Guy Halliwell of the HR Unit said, succeeded in 'getting it off to a good start'. The one substantial change that would be made in repeating the process would be to work more on the barriers that women can face at work and how men and women can work together.

The mentees were not matched with mentors from their own departments. This was seen as essential to the success of the initiative and mentoring as an organizational intervention was not a stated goal, though it has become a result in practice. Mentors and mentees have become more aware of each other's roles and functions within the council and this has directly helped the organizational learning process. The mentoring approach has been important in supporting individuals who may be anxious about being part of major change initiatives that are flattening the management structure and devolving responsibilities. It is the view of the HR Unit at Brent that mentees are coping better with the threat of change because of the mentoring outlet.

Evaluation and Learning

As part of Brent's commitment to Opportunity 2000 and the greater empowerment of women in the workforce, the mentoring initiative at Brent is aimed at a specific target group and designed to achieve a specific result. This concentration on the business case is vitally important. It is not enough to want to undertake mentoring because it's 'pink and fluffy' and everyone is thinking of doing it! The London Borough of Brent has long experience in the field of equal opportunities and is ahead of the field in this area. For the council mentoring represents a leading-edge technique in achieving results in equal opportunities.

So what has come out of this initiative? The existence of the mentoring scheme has improved learning and communication across the council at senior levels. The learning has been a two-way process, with mentors gaining as much as mentees in four key areas:

- It has helped senior managers who are mentors to focus on management development issues.
- It has helped mentors to understand how different parts and levels of the organization think and behave—it cuts down the isolation of top managers.
- Mentors have enjoyed the process—they have enjoyed being looked up to.
- Real working problems/issues have been discussed.

What have mentors needed to think more about?

- Some mentors have not been good at setting an agenda for the relationship.
- There has been a need for more dialogue between the parties to the relationship.
- There has been some disruption to relationships where mentees have not taken the relationship seriously enough.
- Finding the time necessary for the relationship has not been easy in every case. This means that the scheme manager needs to think carefully about people's commitment and their individual workloads when setting up the mentoring pairs.
- No tasks or projects have been set by mentors for mentees to perform. This has helped in managing the boundaries between line managers, mentors and mentees. Mentors need to see that mentees are not an extra project management resource.

One of the key learning points from the Brent experience revolves around the development event for mentors. It is best to orient mentors to the key organizational issues and mechanics of implementing mentoring, rather than including skills training in the same event. Treat skills development as a separate issue and one to be addressed on an individual basis following a development needs analysis. Senior managers particularly may resent a 'sheep-dip' mentoring skills approach.

In the matching process of mentor with mentee, a formal process controlled by HR was favoured. This allowed the wishes of the mentees to be paramount, while not 'wasting' senior managers on too junior mentees where there were obvious skills/job/experience gaps. The process, though formal, was not clinical and allowed scope for the use of knowledge and intuition by HR managers in the matching process. A random 'cocktail party' type of informal event was not pursued as it lacked rigour and could produce embarrassment for those not selected on both sides.

The relationship between line managers, mentors and mentees has been well managed because:

- all parties have been briefed fully on expectations and processes;
- the mentee can only apply for a mentor with the support of the line manager;
- the mentor has not been in 'competition' with the line manager by setting projects for the mentee to complete.

A second tranche of mentees is going well. Brent has doubled the size of the scheme and included junior managers. A mentee training session and handbook have also been introduced.

Some organizations use mentoring for one specific purpose. However, once the strategic approach to mentoring is appreciated, it becomes evident that mentoring can be used across the organization simultaneously for a multitude of different yet complementary business cases. An interesting example of mentoring being used in this way is at BT.

BT

At a one-day conference at the Industrial Society in July 1995, Corina Holmes, then manager of executive development, outlined some of the uses of mentoring within BT. It is an impressive spectrum. It includes mentoring for women, graduates, engineers, masters qualifications, ethnic groups and expatriates in the international sphere.

The core of the BT presentation at the conference was around women and mentoring. BT, a member of the Opportunity 2000 initiative, was keen to increase the quantity and quality of women's participation in the company by sharing strategies that have helped more experienced women managers to overcome barriers to growth and advancement, by creating a network and by promoting the visibility of positive role models.

The management development programme for women started in 1986 and was aimed at enabling them to fulfil their potential. By 1995 600 women had experienced the programme and it had been expanded to four different programmes. Key components of this initiative were to encourage individuals to take responsibilities for the pragmatic implementation of their learning back in the workplace, to transfer that knowledge to encourage others and to act as positive role models for other women in the company.

Mentoring in BT

Mentoring in BT was seen as providing the following:

- Sounding board
- Open doors/access
- Knowledge
- Contacts
- Strategy
- Experience
- Support
- Vision
- Stimulation
- Pave the way to new role.

Mentors

In BT a good mentor is:

- Open
- Respected
- Interested
- A good listener
- Accessible
- Honest
- Professional.

Benefits to mentors

These were seen as:

- Investment in the future
- Sounding board
- Opportunity to reflect
- Opportunity to see projects/dissertation work
- Ego—or feel-good factor
- Giving back
- Seeing the business from a fresh perspective.

The mentoring relationship

This has several elements for consideration by the participants:

- Contracting, issues here include:
  —frequency and duration of meetings;
  —how to use the time;
  —location of meetings;
  —length of the mentoring relationship.
- Developing the relationship
- Redefining the relationship, where necessary
- Ending the relationship
- Mentorees becoming mentors.

Benefits of mentoring to mentorees

Mentorees' 'quotable quotes' include:

- 'Helped me get a new job.'
- 'Managing politics at work.'
- 'Broadening horizons.'
- 'Enjoyable experience.'
- 'Boost for self-esteem.'
- 'I'm in control.'
- 'Growth in confidence.'
- 'Opening doors.'

The BT mentoring initiative has been a significant step towards achieving the company's goal of building a more diverse organization and utilizing its human resources effectively.

SOUTH WEST THAMES REGIONAL HEALTH AUTHORITY

In 1991, the Nursing and Human Resources directorates of South West Thames Regional Health Authority (RHA) decided to set up a mentorship scheme for Grade G nurses within the region. The aim was to see how these nurses could benefit from having a mentor and also to ascertain what organizational lessons could be learned. The region recognized the important contribution of women to healthcare service management and the pivotal role that Grade G nurses play in managing healthcare at 'grass-roots' level. It felt that it was vital to ensure that successful women were given a high profile and to provide the nurses with working examples of successful mentors. It is important to state that Grade G nurses can be male and female.

The programme, which was called 'Stepping Out and Stepping Up' and was the first of its kind in the UK, was launched in January 1992 by Baroness Cumberlege (RHA Chair), with Judith Bryant of the King's Fund College involved as an outside facilitator.

Twenty senior nurses at Epsom Health Care NHS Trust and Frimley Park NHS Trust were mentored by a manager outside their specialism, thereby enabling them to develop and extend their experience. This RHA-led pilot scheme was formally evaluated after only six weeks and as a whole proved to be a success. In the light of this, other units are being encouraged to set up similar schemes.

The SW Thames Definition of Mentoring

A mentor is an experienced, trusted adviser. In a mentoring partnership, a mentor may act as a counsellor, coach, friend or trusted confidant to assist the personal and career development of a partner. Preceptorship, however, is a term commonly used in the nursing profession to imply a relationship which involves teaching, assessing and supervising a more junior member of staff.

Objectives of the Mentoring Scheme

The 'Stepping Out and Stepping Up' pilot was one of a number of RHA and national initiatives (e.g. Opportunity 2000) to ensure that women in the NHS develop their potential to the full. The aims of the programme were to select a group of ambitious and committed nurses and help them to develop skills outside their usual area of work and to extend their management experience. Both the nurses and their mentors would be given the opportunity to improve their skills and to acquire new ones. The aim was for them to achieve confidence and a better awareness of themselves, their organizations, their strengths and their development needs. Mentors would also gain a better understanding of what nurses actually do.

The programme was designed to:

- be a positive and stimulating experience for all;
- break down occupational barriers;
- help each individual to grow both personally and professionally.

Because it was the first of its kind, the pilot scheme and its evaluation would provide a valuable opportunity for data collection and research.

Mentors and Nurses

Twenty female nurses in grade G, working as ward sisters, community district nurses or health visitors at Frimley Park Hospital Trust and Epsom Health Care Trust, took part in the programme. They were assigned a mentor chosen from a range of NHS occupations unrelated to nursing and in a more senior management position within the same unit. The matching process was done at each location by the personnel function, exercising judgement based on their knowledge of the participants. The mentors were chosen from volunteers.

The mentors, 65% women and 35% men, included a pharmacist, a physiotherapist, an accountant, two medical laboratory scientific officers, personnel managers, a chartered engineer and a non-executive board member. The project was sponsored at Epsom by Margaret Soo, the Trust matron, and at Frimley Park by Janet King, director of personnel.

The Process

It was felt that developing a meaningful relationship is important for a mentoring partnership. The critical factor was the development of mutual trust and confidence. There were three stages to the partnership:

- forming the relationship;
- working together in partnership;
- concluding the relationship.

It was decided that the needs, aspirations and expectations must clearly be defined from the outset. Time commitments have to be mapped out—this is particularly relevant in a patient-centred environment when the unexpected is most likely to happen. The partners met once a week, at least. The line managers of partners being mentored must be fully briefed because their encouragement and help are vital components in the success of the mentoring relationship. It is important to acknowledge that the relationship will at some stage conclude, be it by a job change or by mutual agreement. In this programme, when the pilot came to an end officially at the end of six weeks, 19 out of 20 partnerships elected to continue their relationships.

Two highly interactive briefing workshops were held to give the nurses (independently) and their mentors an opportunity to explore the concepts of mentoring and understand what they could get out of the programme. Facilitators from the King's Fund College took the groups through some basic learning and management development concepts. Relationships were formed and plans made during the briefing workshops. The couples met on a regular basis and in some cases mentors 'shadowed' their nurse partners. Thoughts and feelings were recorded in individual diaries.

The nurses and their mentors met with regional coordinators on two separate evenings to swap experiences and provide feedback. The evaluation of the pilot project was in the form of continuous assessment, briefing and evaluation workshops, individual feedback, reflective diaries and questionnaires. At the end of the pilot a social event was held for everyone concerned with the programme. Throughout the pilot, a telephone 'hotline' staffed by two personnel advisers was operated by the RHA.

What Were the Benefits of the Programme?

The nurses experienced a broader view of the organization and themselves. As one said: 'As nurses we are very clinical and prescriptive . . .we tend to see ourselves as very important. We now know that there are lots of other people who are equally important and can see the pressures that other people in the hospital are under.' Self-confidence has been given a boost and innovative ways of working have been developed. Cross-functional working outside of hierarchies has improved.

Teamworking

Teamworking across organizational boundaries has improved. These senior nurses now know more about other work in the hospital. One developed new computer skills, another set up a joint initiative with health promotion, one nurse's improved understanding of HR issues has enabled her to work more closely with the personnel function to sort out staffing and workload concerns. On the other hand, the mentors said that the relationships had broadened their horizons and that they felt that they learned as much as their partners.

Personal skills

Many Grade G nurses felt more assertive, with a desire to improve the way they work. As one said: 'I make lists of things to do today. . . . I get letters typed. . . . I say what I want . . . and am now prepared to confront people. . . . I didn't feel like this before.'

Improved lines of communication

The mentorship programme has provided some sense of organizational purpose to communication and considerably opened up dialogue between staff groups and departments.

A chance to 'unload'

The established trust of the relationship enabled nurses to offload accumulated negative feelings and to look for solutions to problems.

Time for personal development

The programme had in itself provided opportunities to look at participants' own clinical and working practices. 'Mentoring has endorsed the importance of having time and space at work—to be an innovator.'

Line manager support

For the scheme to be successful, it was felt that line managers must be involved from the outset in giving encouragement and support. Their help is particularly important in setting aside time from work duties for mentors and nurses to meet. The two main barriers to a successful and ongoing relationship were a lack of time and the stress relating to the perception of leaving colleagues to cope in the absence of the nurse being mentored.

Management development

Women in the organization are more aware of the opportunities that could be available for personal development in the future. The project has improved skills analysis—what the nurses have and what they need to develop.

Managing and decision making

The project has encouraged the nurses to seek a wider role in the management and decision-making processes of the hospitals.

Only one failure

Of the 20 mentoring pairs, only one failed, apparently because the partners said that the mentoring process did not meet their expectations. The majority found the programme valuable in extending themselves in the workplace.

Post-Programme Developments

At Frimley Park Hospital, the mentoring scheme has been extended to cover people who are engaged on a course of study leading to a qualification. The mentors come from a wide variety of professional backgrounds, both medical and managerial. Providing mentors for new recruits has helped in induction and reduced staff turnover. Mentoring has also enabled senior management to get access to the abilities of younger managers.

Janet King, HR director at Frimley, sees the role of the mentor as being:

- to coach;
- to counsel;
- to listen and enthuse;
- to motivate;
- to be impartial but to have empathy with individuals;
- often to be an 'ideas' person and sponsor.

King feels that impartiality is a prime quality for a mentor, in order to take a non-directive approach to the mentoring relationship. The mentor should also be non-judgemental as opposed to exercising judgement! She feels that one of the difficulties of the counselling role is that it becomes difficult to separate the private/personal issues from the workplace ones. This needs to be discussed fully between the participants at the 'contract' stage. One potential danger to be avoided is the mentoring relationship degenerating into a 'gossip' session. The mentors in this programme have tended to be in their mid-forties, with the nurses in their twenties and thirties.

At Epsom Hospital, the scheme has moved on to encompass junior doctors who are new to Epsom. The mentors once again are managers and other senior medical staff. The objective is to provide the doctors with more personal support, as they have clinical tutors who are senior consultants. Of the doctors, 60–70% are graduates of St George's Hospital, London, which operates a mentoring scheme. The one at Epsom is seen as continuing that support.

One of the main problems in achieving full success for this scheme has been the very real lack of available time on the part of the junior doctors themselves. This issue of time, together with geography—mentors and mentorees having access to one another—is a significant challenge for some organizations. In 1994, the plan was changed to match up junior doctors as mentorees with experienced ward sisters, many of whom will have been mentorees themselves, to get around some of these problems.

WOMEN AND THE MENTORING RELATIONSHIP

There are some significant learning points that can be drawn from the experience of organizations who engage in mentoring to assist the development of women:

- Women may face different problems to men in mentoring relationships.
- A mentor can significantly accelerate a woman's professional development compared to that of other women without mentors.
- It has been said in the US that women in mentoring relationships have greater job satisfaction than women without mentors.
- Men are likely to be mentors to women.
- Women mentors are in short supply at very senior level.
- The gender of the mentor is less important to success than their quality as mentors.
- The mentor should be aware of their own style and behaviour and those of the mentoree.
- Mentors and mentorees must be aware of the potential for attraction and beware of the dangers of starting an 'affair'. This, of course, need not apply only in cross-gender situations.
- Participants need to be prepared to counter office gossip and jealousies.
- Mentors are important in introducing women to the organization's power structure, formal and informal.
- Women and their potential mentors require specific preparation for their role, particularly in awareness of the psychological/social barriers that can inhibit progress.
- The issue of exploitation or sexual harassment needs to be addressed as part of the preparation for any mentoring programme.

MENTORING AND MINORITY GROUPS

It is true to say that there has been less work done in the area of mentoring for minority groups within organizations. However, organizations such as Marks and Spencer and the UK Customs and Excise have used mentoring schemes in this area, aimed at boosting the recruitment of minorities (*People Development*, 14 March 1995). Managers at retailers WH Smith act as mentors to students from ethnic minorities as part of its management development strategy. Instead of using mentoring in the recruitment process, the aim is to increase awareness of equal opportunities among managers and to help them to develop appropriate mentoring skills.

In 1990, the London Borough of Lewisham set up its 'sponsor scheme', intended to help increase the diversity of managers employed by the authority. It is a voluntary scheme and, after an interview, sponsee/applicants' development needs are assessed by the HR function and they are given access to a list of relevant mentors, called sponsors. The framework of the relationship is worked out at a meeting between the mentoree, mentor and HR representative. The benefits have been those usually associated with mentoring schemes generally, for example confidence building, increased networking and career development benefits. Much of the success of the scheme has derived from the fact that this was seen as a strategic organizational initiative with the subsequent involvement of senior management. Best practice in implementation, including workshops and good supporting literature, has ensured a successful result for Lewisham.

The value of mentoring in assisting the development of diversity in organizations cannot be overstated, so long as one does not regard mentoring as the only thing that has to be done. As with all the other applications of mentoring in the organizational context, success depends on dovetailing the mentoring part of the initiative with other strategic developmental approaches. This is evident particularly in the way that BT, for example, has chosen to proceed. Mentoring can inhabit those areas of the organizational culture where many things are hidden or unclear. It is a perfect tool for understanding the unwritten and often unacknowledged parts of organizational thought and behaviour. Mentoring relationships can provide a safe environment where many of the more difficult issues surrounding organizational life can be challenged and dealt with positively.

Chapter 7

Mentoring and Graduate Development

Developing newly recruited graduates and trainees occasions the most frequent use of mentoring in the organizational context. However, mentoring goes back much further in the education system and is to be found in schools, colleges, universities and in teacher training and development. A key difference between mentoring for young people in further education and in organizations is the issue of assessment. In further education a mentor is often appointed to help the student with their academic progress. That mentor is often part of the formal appraisal process. As we have said, the concept of using a mentor as an assessor of the mentoree militates against the establishment of a full mentoring relationship. The consequence of bringing into the relationship the element of assessment immediately changes the dynamics and can lead to a good relationship, but possibly not one in which there is complete openness by the participants. When designing an organizational scheme for newly recruited graduates, it is vital to ascertain who in the group has had a mentor at college or university and to reassure them that in this new context the mentor will not be part of any assessment process.

Graduate schemes are of several different types. In the first place there is the relatively small-scale approach which is highly focused and qualitatively and quantitatively of central importance to the organization's management succession scenario in the relatively short term. Secondly, a larger-scale, 'lower-key' but important mentoring scheme may support the larger-scale recruitment scenario. This needs big numbers to fulfil operational needs but is talent spotting for the top. It is by nature more diluted and less immediately of central impact and importance to management succession. This is not to say that in the larger scheme, which is often seen as less radical and underpinning a graduate recruitment and development scheme, the high flyers cannot be ascertained.

What we have here are two different but equally valid types of organizational mentoring for newly recruited graduates. They are suited directly to the needs and nature of diverse businesses such as Kingfisher plc, Europe's largest retailer, and LIFFE, the London International Financial Futures and Options Exchange, the second largest futures market in the world, built from scratch in 15 years.

KINGFISHER PLC

Kingfisher, led by chief executive Sir Geoffrey Mulcahy, is the UK's leading retailer, incorporating such household names as Woolworth, B&Q, Superdrug and Comet, and has sales of around £6.5 billion. Kingfisher is becoming a force in global retailing, for example the company has a substantial presence in France where it owns, among other companies, Darty, the market-leading electrical retailer.

Kingfisher takes the development of its people very seriously and has in place a sophisticated and effective graduate recruitment and development scheme, called Kingfisher Management Development Scheme (KMDS). The format of the scheme pivots around three concepts that support one another. The first is a real job within the organization, as opposed to low-key, low-added-value assignments. The concept of the real job means that there is an immediate contribution to and impact on the business by graduate recruits from day one. The second part of the KMDS involves a formal programme of learning in cooperation with an external education provider, which underpins on-the-job experience with learning at incremental levels from DMS studies to MBA. The organization emphasizes that this element of the KMDS is as important as any other. The final of the three elements is mentoring. Each of the graduates is allocated a mentor to assist with integration and ongoing development. The directors are typically at senior management and director levels. The KMDS is a group initiative and is managed centrally, although the graduates have appointments in the constituent businesses. The role of mentoring has been seen by both mentors and mentorees as central to the success of the KMDS.

The mentors and mentorees received development opportunities prior to the mentoring element being launched. Key messages to the mentors were that any extra background information on mentorees that could be supplied to mentors would be given appropriately. Also, mentors could visit graduates 'in the field' but proper handling of this would be vital by both mentors and mentorees. Kingfisher scheme managers were concerned by the potentially negative impact that a close mentoring relationship, let alone an unannounced visit by a very senior manager or director, could have on the graduates' other working relationships. For this reason, it was felt that mentors need to have a positive relationship with the graduates' line managers, but also need to be impartial 'champions' to whom their graduates can turn, as it is acknowledged that mentors are important safety valves for graduates.

One of the drivers for introducing mentoring to support the graduate programme was the importance of the retention issue and it was decided that, where possible, mentors should ideally meet potential trainees as part of the recruitment process and should have a say in the best placements for their mentorees. They were not involved in the matching process itself, but due consideration was given to the seniority of mentors and their position in the business in relation to the graduate.

Matching using knowledge of the 'softer' information (background, interests, same university where appropriate) was attempted and well received. Also, physical distance is an important factor in matching the relationship. The KMDS mentors were actively encouraged to agree their 'agenda' with the graduate as soon as possible and were fully briefed on all aspects of the scheme. The use of other, more experienced graduates as 'buddies' for the new intake was considered and encouraged. This was seen as getting an extra bite at the cherry in helping people to settle into the organization.

In many organizations, opinion is often divided on the advantages and disadvantages of having personnel or HR people as mentors. This is a difficult issue, as these people are often superbly equipped to perform the role of mentors. There was no policy about this at Kingfisher and a number of HR people were involved as mentors. However, it may be appropriate in some organizations to use HR personnel as advisers to the mentoring scheme rather than as mentors.

The line managers of the graduates probably needed more understanding of what was involved in the mentoring relationship as no mentoring development was scheduled. However, all the line managers were thoroughly briefed on the workings of the KMDS and it was felt to be part of the responsibility of the graduates to bring their line managers up to speed on what mentoring was about. It is important not to exclude the line management of mentorees when setting up a mentoring initiative.

Some of the learning from the KMDS can be summarized briefly. It was felt that regular contact between the mentors and mentorees must happen. The less successful relationships had less contact. The reasons were lack of motivation from some mentors and lack of time and/or opportunity. The

KMDS managers received feedback that early communication to mentors and mentorees about the match is important and this suggestion was incorporated for future graduate entries. There was a view expressed that some first meetings between mentors and graduates were perceived as being too formal and work has been done to rectify this. What has emerged is that the career development role of the mentor is prized by mentorees and that the recruitment process will, where possible, actively involve the future mentor population and produce even more understanding of the role and hence more commitment among the KMDS mentors.

A survey of the main benefits to the mentorees showed the following results. Graduates felt that mentoring is important in confidence building, producing impartial advice and reminds graduates of 'what they are there for'. They felt that mentoring adds weight to the KMDS, gives them better organizational understanding, ongoing personal support which helps clarify their role and has been invaluable in generating future career development advice.

A similar survey of the views of mentors produced some interesting results. Some mentors saw the mentoring relationship with a new graduate as an opportunity to see the world through fresh and perhaps naïve eyes and enjoyed being challenged on perceived wisdom. Many mentors felt that they had obtained a clearer view of impact of the organizational management style of the component companies and had a better understanding of some of the organizational issues exercising others in the company. Some said that mentoring had improved their own management style and found that mentoring provided an opportunity to stop and reflect on the business. All this is very welcome when we remember that the main organizational purposes for introducing mentoring were to improve the retention of valuable graduate recruits, the induction of these new people and the ongoing career development of the graduates as well as providing personal support for individuals.

While it is true to say that most benefit has been received by the graduates in this mentoring initiative, the mentors individually and collectively have indicated that they have seen the process as two way and have benefited from their contact with the graduates.

One mentor very positively admitted that being a mentor had changed his management style towards the team of individuals reporting to him. There was less command/control and a more facilitative and open style. Mentors reported a clearer view of what it is like to be both new to the organization and starting at the 'bottom' again. There was a view that the ultimate impact of the organization's management style and the decisions could be seen more clearly by mentors. One mentor gave an example of a decision taken at top level that had an unintended and almost opposite effect when it was finally implemented. Another mentor said: 'Mentoring is good at keeping my eyes open.' Thus organizational communication has been improved among the group involved in the mentoring scheme.

The opportunity to reflect on the decisions and conduct of organizational life is noted by many mentors. Talking through issues with graduates has often brought real benefits and mentors themselves have bounced ideas off graduates, though not always necessarily very obviously. The graduates' fresh perspective has proved useful to mentors. Graduates have challenged the mentors throughout the mentoring process to justify the ways of the organization and this has resulted positively in the mentors becoming change agents and advocates of doing things differently and better.

Evaluating Success at Kingfisher

The approach of evaluation has been a series of semi-structured interviews with a sample of mentors and mentorees from across the operating companies. The interview format was intended to question common elements, but at the same time to allow interviewees an opportunity to raise their issues spontaneously. The general structure covered the following areas:

- What was your general view of the scheme? Have you changed your mind about anything?
- How was the 'process' (training etc.) handled? How was your mentoring partner's training handled?
- How were your expectations handled? Your partner's?
- What problems have you experienced?
- Comments on the matching process?
- What are the benefits of mentoring to you? Your partner?
- What would you do differently and why?
- Any other comments?

No one expressed a view that mentoring was unnecessary or resented it. The mentorees, most of whom had no previous experience of mentoring, considered that the career development side of mentoring is a key benefit and some mentorees suggested 'advertising' mentoring early on as part of the recruitment process. It was suggested that it should rate a key mention in the Kingfisher brochure. Some mentors had previous experience of being involved in mentoring, as both mentors and mentorees.

Many mentorees found the influence of the mentors beneficial in addressing 'grey areas' that cropped up from time to time. They felt that it was important to have 'someone to go to' to help with interpreting things and found positive assistance with working through the graduate portfolio. Mentors were seen as providing help with questions such as: 'What should be my next placement?' Or 'How do I go about this?' They felt that impartiality was a key characteristic of their mentors.

Some mentorees expressed the view that they did not know what to expect from their individual mentors, but were aware that it was up to them to contribute to setting the guidelines and parameters of their mentoring relationships. They felt that they needed to spend time thinking about how to approach their mentors for the first time.

Mentors should spend time thinking about their graduates and particularly not assume too much knowledge and understanding on their part. Some mentorees felt that mentors need to realize how little new recruits really know and understand.

Many mentorees felt that the choice of store placement was crucial and that it may be an idea to involve the mentor more in this process. There are organizational sensitivities in this situation, particularly from line managers, where mentors are visiting graduates in store, especially where the mentors are very senior. Some mentors visited the graduates in the store and some did not. In some cases the mentoree was involved in long journeys for relatively short meetings. The whole area of distance should be revisited for future graduate intakes. Where both mentors and graduates are in head office locations, there tends to be a more informal, 'drop-in' policy. Some difficulties occur in this regard at the in-store stage.

KMDS mentors have resisted the challenge of trying to solve the problems of the graduates directly. Their approach was constructive and addressed the needs of the graduates while simultaneously not infringing the organization's line relationships. Mentors have acted to alleviate real problems in the graduate mentorees, particularly in their in-store experiences. There were no reported lapses in the area of confidentiality between mentors and mentorees.

Both parties to the relationship made the point that they felt early matching and communication of the match was important. Some mentorees felt that they met their mentors a little late and mentors should realize that it is important to contact their graduates as a matter of priority. Mentors felt that any additional background information on the graduates would be welcome and would help to start off the relationship successfully. This information would include potential placements and career development issues. Graduates will need different levels of support, but everyone appreciates the need to commence the mentoring relationship on a positive note.

Many mentors expressed the view that the first meeting should be held away from the workplace. Mentors and mentorees felt that they were available to talk at any time and that the frequency would be driven by the needs of the graduates. A minority of graduates said that they felt that it was hard to arrange meetings with their mentors. Mentors may need to communicate to their own support staff the importance of the mentoring relationship and the KMDS graduates' access. Mentors and mentorees need to structure their first meeting well. Mentors and mentorees would ideally like to see cooperation between the line manager and the mentor and to agree common goals for the development of the graduate.

The fact that senior managers within Kingfisher are mentors adds weight to the KMDS. They are seen by graduates as champions of their group and able to influence the organization positively to enable graduates to be more effective in their roles.

For many graduates their mentors play a useful task in keeping them focused. The mentor can help the graduate to balance the demands of the different component elements of the KMDS. The mentoring element of the KMDS is working and is seen as central to its success. Both mentors and mentorees have put energy and enthusiasm into making the mentoring relationships work. They have all done it differently and in their own way. However, the work that the Kingfisher centre has done in laying good foundations for the mentoring scheme has been a vital ingredient in its success.

LONDON INTERNATIONAL FINANCIAL FUTURES AND OPTIONS EXCHANGE (LIFFE)

LIFFE is part of an industry which provides an efficient and cost-effective way for financial institutions to manage their exposure to financial and other risks. LIFFE provides an international exchange for its members (around 200 banks and financial organizations) to trade financial and commodity derivatives by live calling and electronic trading. LIFFE also has the responsibility for regulating the market and its own members, as well as creating new financial products to be traded. The organization has come into existence and grown over only 15 years to be the second largest such market after Chicago. London's time zone—between the US, Europe and the Far East—has certainly contributed to its competitive edge, but it has also been the professionalism, experience and 'can do' culture of the employees of the Exchange which have led the way to success.

In order that business can continue to grow successfully, the Exchange has, particularly over the last four years, had a sophisticated graduate recruitment and development scheme. The profile of the graduates recruited by LIFFE differs from that of some other organizations in that the Exchange's recruits are often older, with work experience and some with higher degrees, though in fact some people do join directly from university. There is fierce competition for the dozen places usually available, with 100 applications for each position. Thus LIFFE is fortunate in having a wide selection of potential recruits of high quality. Unfortunately, the environment into which these people are recruited is highly competitive and highly rewarded and in the past the Exchange has suffered some attrition in the job market—ironically often from its own members. It was thought that something 'extra' was needed to underpin the graduate scheme to ensure the retention of people whom the Exchange valued. The concept of mentoring was explored as one of the options to fulfil this need.

A second organizational reason for the introduction of mentoring was the desire to provide the graduates with personal support. As we have said, LIFFE is a highly sophisticated and complex environment in which to work with many diverse functions. The graduates are in the position of being employed centrally by the Exchange but, within 12 months, after having had experience in different parts of the Exchange, they have to find themselves a 'perch' in the organization. This could be in the business development function, information technology, regulation or any of the other constituent functions of the Exchange. It was felt that a mentor could aid this process by getting a graduate up to speed more quickly. The idea was not for the initiative to become a patronage model where the mentor finds the graduate a job, but was much more about being an extra resource to the graduate, helping them get to grips with the culture of the organization.

Implementing Mentoring

Design

The process of implementing mentoring at LIFFE had two stages. The first involved designing the mentoring scheme itself. The first objective was to profile and select the mentors. There was considerable discussion about this question, as the choice of mentors would in the LIFFE environment make or break the initiative. It was realized that there was only one chance: it had to work first time. Volunteers were therefore sought from the population of directors and senior management team to become mentors to the graduates.

The seniority of mentors will have various impacts on any mentoring initiative. There are several schools of thought. If very senior managers and directors are used, is this a waste of their valuable time and expertise? The answer has to be that it depends on the organizational objective of the mentoring initiative and also on the level of the mentorees. It may well be a perfectly good idea to use junior or middle managers for mentoring graduates. It is fair to say that coaching schemes frequently tend to have participants nearer in level in organizational terms. However, in the case of LIFFE several factors contributed to the overall view that most impact would result from using senior people in the role of mentor. The first is the exceptional quality of the mentorees and a desire on the part of the organization to show how much they were valued. The second factor involves the reinforcement of mentoring in a positive way within the Exchange. Mentoring would be a new concept and to indicate its importance the directors and senior management could send a very positive signal to the organization and help to start moving the organizational culture in the desired direction. Lastly, LIFFE values a meritocratic management approach—what you achieve gains respect. While they would not be typecast as role models, the involvement of respected senior management was seen as beneficial to the launch and implementation of the scheme as well as to its long-term success.

The matching process was then the subject of careful consideration and debate. As we have seen, there is no foolproof or scientific way of matching up mentors and their partners. In the case of LIFFE, there were some organizational constraints in that it was decided that it would not be appropriate to match a mentoree with a mentor who was responsible for the performance of the graduate or had any direct working relationship that could inhibit the mentoring processes. Once this had been worked out, pairings were suggested by the HR function which was managing the scheme. These pairings were communicated first to the mentors, to confirm that there were no operational reasons for the match not being made. This was a practical check and also involved the mentors quite early on in the mentoring initiative, helping to build commitment and enthusiasm. After this, the knowledge of both sets of participants guided a 'gut feel' approach to matching people together.

One of the most important features of the LIFFE mentoring scheme was the decision to employ a 'no fault' get-out clause for both mentors and graduates. This meant that either party to the mentoring relationship could end it as a matter of right, without explanations being required. This was intended to make it possible to end mentoring quickly and cleanly, without offence to anyone, if circumstances warranted it. As we have said, mentoring is a relationship and not a process. It is easy to underestimate the importance of personal 'chemistry' and no amount of rationalization will overcome dislike between people.

The get-out clause is very useful with new graduates. In the first place, as people are totally new to each other there is little information to go on and a lack of empathy can develop between the participants, particularly where they find out that they have little in common on which to base their mentoring relationship. Fortunately, this is rare in these circumstances. However, the extra good news is that as the graduate is 'brand new', there is no organizational history and baggage to be brought to the relationship. We are often obliged to work with people towards whom we may have little liking and empathy and we make an effort accordingly. It is after all a useful organizational and social skill to be able to get on with all types of people. Nevertheless, in terms of protecting the mentoring scheme, it is sensible to have this get-out option—and to manage it proactively if a problem occurs— as both participants have confidence that if they do not hit it off, or the mentor feels that they have less time than they anticipated to be a mentor, at least the mentoring can be brought to an end positively. Whether or not one reassigns a mentoree in this situation will very often depend on the individual circumstances involved. At LIFFE no one wished or needed to use this option, but people felt that it was a good idea to have it on offer as an added protection for everyone concerned.

One of the greatest challenges to successful mentoring in organizations is that of time. The culture and operational life of the Exchange, like that of many other organizations, is one of high pressure and time constraints. It was felt that it was right to be up front with mentors about the extra time that was needed. Without exception, the mentors understood and committed to giving sufficient time to making mentoring work. However, it was made clear to the graduates that time was an issue for mentors and they should be careful of not appearing indifferent to this, particularly when arranging or rearranging meetings. Having said this, the evaluation revealed that with one exception—a mentor who had an extremely high international travel burden—the time constraints did not prove insurmountable for the mentoring partners.

The mentoring relationships were designed to last up to 12 months. If a mentoring relationship ended, then a pragmatic decision about re-matching would take place. One mentoring relationship came to an end because the graduate went to work directly with the mentor and they both decided to end the formal relationship. The mentoree felt that he had formed a network of contacts and became busy building other relationships to compensate for the formal ending of the mentoring relationship. In this circumstance, the mentor and mentoree had developed a good and lasting relationship which in turn helped to produce an open and productive line relationship.

Examining possible challenges to the mentoring initiative, it was felt that there should be a frank approach to discussing what mentoring involved if people without mentors queried the scheme. It was considered important to present mentoring as an integral part of the strategy that had been mapped out for the graduates' development. However, it was decided not to launch mentoring to the wider organization at this stage. Any questions about mentoring from other staff would be dealt with on an individual basis in the normal way. As it happens, there was no adverse reaction to the mentoring initiative from people not on the graduate programme.

One of the most important factors in the process of implementation was gaining support for the scheme. Fortunately, the chief executive and board of LIFFE were very quickly persuaded of the benefits of the approach. One of the key reasons for this was a very businesslike lobbying process orchestrated by the HR mentoring scheme managers, which concentrated on the overall strategic organizational benefits to be gained. The approach was seen as relevant and sharply focused, with some deliverable objectives in terms of the retention and development of the graduate cadre.

Training

Stage two of the process of implementation revolved around 'training' the mentors and graduates. A half-day event was designed for the mentor group and one for the graduates. The mentors' workshop was timed to be held first, as this enabled the scheme managers to pick up any unforeseen issues from this important group of participants. Also, it enabled the expectations and views of the mentors to be elicited and communicated anonymously as a list to the graduates. This proved a powerful exercise, as both groups were not just asked for their expectations of mentoring but also to say what they thought the other group's expectations would be. It was possible in the case of the graduates to let them compare what was actually said by the mentors to what they imagined those expectations to be.

The main concerns of the mentors were:

- How will the mentoring scheme affect my staff?
- How will it affect my relationship with the graduate's line manager?
- Will I have time to do this justice?
- What happens if the relationship fails?
- How will I be allocated a graduate?
- How confidential will the relationship be?

There was also a rather fun session in the mentors' event which asked them about their expectations of the graduates. The replies were both instructive and amusing:

- Enthusiasm
- 'The right attitude!'
- Initiative
- Realism
- Intelligence
- Commitment
- Understanding the contract between them.

Although this caused some amusement, it was useful in providing an agenda to enable the graduate group to examine some of the realities of organizational life.

The graduates had their revenge, which certainly gave the mentors something to think about. They wanted help with:

- knowledge of the organization;

- motivation, encouragement and assistance in setting career goals;
- interpretation of situations and events in the organization;

together with:

- objectivity and confidentiality;
- an open and frank relationship.

The Results

The development events were facilitated, using internal and external facilitators, and were pragmatic, non-academic and based on the live issues of the participants. The approach was judged to be a success by both mentors and mentorees. There was no development event directly for the line managers, who had been informed of the mentoring initiative, but it was felt that the graduates should take the initiative and responsibility for informing their managers about how mentoring was working for them without, of course, breaching the strict rule about maintaining confidentiality regarding the content of their mentoring conversations.

The results of the graduate mentoring initiative at LIFFE show that it has fulfilled its objectives and business case. The organization has retained its graduates in the face of stiff competition at a level that has exceeded best-guess expectations. The graduates themselves have moved quickly into mainstream jobs within the Exchange. In addition, the mentors have indicated that they have benefited from the mentoring relationships. Finally, the Exchange is now actively examining ways of further extending the benefits of mentoring into the organization. The planning and implementation of the graduate mentoring scheme at LIFFE is an example of excellence and best practice in the field of organizational mentoring.

Chapter 8

Mentoring and Change

At its most strategic level, a mentoring initiative is really all about change. Very often organizations are looking for ways of improving their competitive edge by getting their people to interact more efficiently and effectively in the context of all sorts of business cases.

The main problem faced by organizations addressing change is transforming those habits of mind that have been framed by earlier events or scenarios. How do we get people to stop and examine what they are doing at work? Organizations also face the challenge of dealing with rapidly moving events. Technology has been a blessing and a curse in this respect, as things can now move very quickly indeed. This gives less time for reflection in decision making and organizations prize swift but effective decision makers. Recent management surveys in the UK have unfortunately suggested that what cause deep stress to individuals are not only remote decision making by senior managers, but constant delays in taking decisions. Can it be that there is a real lack of confidence or even competence in the management ranks? In any event, how can we help to change this type of mindset?

Possibly one of the things that might help to improve the process and quality of decision making would be regular opportunities to step outside of the frame and look at the main issues facing us as individual managers in organizations. Many managers have been forced by the speed of events to develop highly activist styles of management (activist does not necessarily equate with speed in this context). Mentoring, if properly thought out, is not the *only* answer to this, but it can help to underpin change in this context. Many managers testify that having a mentor has helped them to take a realistic view of their contribution at work and their place in the organization.

This mentoring approach can be used in conjunction with coaching to achieve the desired changes to levels of competence and the way work is handled. This in itself is a major contributory factor in reducing levels of stress for busy managers. Managing ambiguity in the organizational context is a major life skill or competency that can be helped to grow by the judicious use of mentoring as an approach.

In some organizations the organizational structure can militate against effective communication and integration between members of the workforce. Where this is perceived as a problem, there may be conditions that make it very difficult to change this environmental 'given'. In these cases, people start to look for ways of working around the problem. This is not to say that organizational mentoring is subversive in nature—often the reverse is true—but it can help to alleviate some of the problems caused in organizations by such things as structures. Forming good mentoring relationships across the organization can contribute to building effective networks and greater managerial effectiveness.

The concept of the learning organization is one which has been debated for years by managers, practitioners of management development and management writers. Whatever definition one cares to apply, there is little doubt that effective mentoring relationships can enhance the process of sharing knowledge and understanding—dare one say learning—in organizations. As learning is often generated from change, the periodic opportunity of reflection that is offered by the discipline of a structured mentoring relationship can highlight, fix and enhance that learning.

Culture change is very much an area where mentoring can assist organizations and individuals. When change is occurring in organizations, several different things are happening at once. There is a passive scenario where there may or may not be an awareness that the current organizational scenario is being affected by an external stimulus or that there has been a change in the direction or operation of the organization. An example could be an innovation by a major competitor which in turn causes an organization to respond in an *ad hoc* way in its own operations. No one has stated that the problem exists and that there is no strategic answer to it, but the organization is responding nevertheless. This scenario will inevitably cause stresses among employees who are going through transition in response to the change. Another form of change is more active in focus. One instance could be the environment in which an organization operates, for example a change in the law bringing deregulation to an industry sector. In this circumstance, there is more warning of impending change and organizations can be more proactive in planning to meet that change. Of course, several types of change can be happening simultaneously and this can have implications for the business case for mentoring and the type of scheme to be introduced.

To illustrate some of these different scenarios, two real-life studies from the financial services sector are offered. This sector has been transformed totally over the last decade. The deregulation of the marketplace has changed building societies into banks and those that remained as building societies are now offering many more services in banking and insurance. Many of the old distinctions have disappeared in the way stock exchanges function and, as we saw in the previous chapter, some businesses have been newly invented and come to international prominence within this time. Globalization and the opening up of new markets have brought new players and fresh competition. Mergers and acquisitions have altered the landscape of our high streets and the financial centres of the world. Meanwhile the effects of privatization of formerly state-controlled enterprises mean that for the first time in the UK, we have a large shareholding public who are ever more discriminating and sophisticated in their choice of financial services and products. This has had an enormous impact on the way financial services companies organize themselves and do business.

Many of the managers in these organizations had been recruited under the old scenario and were now being asked not only to change actively their way of doing business but to develop, very quickly, new competencies to meet the new demands of the marketplace. This was very much the background for the first organizational mentoring example given here, Company Y. Our second example, Company X, shows how mentoring can be used in the workplace to enhance and underpin a learning culture which is still going through the kind of changes that have just been described.

COMPANY Y

This building society with assets of several billion pounds sterling is one of the largest UK building societies. It has a large branch network with several thousand employees. The last few years have been a period of rapid change, particularly following the arrival of a new chief executive in 1989. The society's vision is to become a major UK retailer of financial services and it has pursued a strategy of diversification around its core business. In 1990, it commenced an ambitious project to develop a network of large financial centres, offering customers an integrated range of services, the first of which opened in 1991. To support this project, it was recognized that the society would need to develop a new customer service culture and set of values and that the entire management population would need to be mobilized in its development.

An organizational analysis carried out in 1990 concluded that as the society changed from a traditional building society to a financial services retailer, the effect of rapid change and more demanding goals and standards has produced a demand for adequate training and support. As the report of the analysis said: 'These changes taken together have produced . . . a shock wave and eagerness for growth among most management.'

In looking at the alternatives and solutions from the organizational analysis, the society affirmed its intention to develop and grow its own people. Mentoring offered the greatest potential to provide a timely and fundamental change in culture and to support staff in a period of change.

The solution was a two-year organizational development project comprising three elements:

- zero-error service programme
- developing a customer relationship programme
- mentoring programme.

The mentoring programme, also a two-year project, was designed as a key part of a comprehensive approach to change management. The programme had three initial objectives which were communicated at briefings and in writing to participants:

1. To assist the society in achieving its organizational vision of becoming a prime financial services retailer, through ensuring that employees have the maximum opportunity for career growth and recognition.
2. To teach the pilot population of mentees how to become effective mentors themselves, so that the mentoring philosophy and process becomes the primary leadership style of the society.
3. To increase the performance of the society as a whole and of individual mentees by 25%. Thus the mentoring programme was designed to provide both a framework for organizational growth and a vehicle for performance improvement.

Mentors and Mentees

The day-to-day management of the project and mentor supervision were provided by an external consultancy which had operated mentoring programmes in the US. The mentors were external consultants. The project reported to the head of the HR function and was coordinated by a specially created training and mentoring department within the society.

The programme started with 168 mentees and ended with 205. The mentees were defined as the total management population and selection was automatic.

The mentors (between 15 and 25 mentees per mentor) were employed by or contracted to the consultancy to work on a full-time basis. They were selected on the basis of previous psychological training and business management experience, together with good interpersonal skills, integrity and a personal commitment to their own continuous development in order to act as a role model to mentees. The mentors received training in the consultancy's mentoring model prior to commencement of mentoring and the model employed required considerable skills on their part. Mentors had their own confidential resource, to provide them with unconditional support in the form of the mentoring supervisor, who was distinct from the project management process. External mentors were employed to provide skills which the organization did not possess internally and also to ease the impact that the use of internal mentors would pose.

In addition, it was felt that the mentoring relationship needed to be outside the line relationship. Mentors and mentees were matched by division but, where moves occurred, they remained in the original relationship. Meetings were weekly for one hour but other arrangements could be made where necessary. Withdrawal from the programme was possible following the agreement of a mentee's line manager and interview with the mentoring supervisor. However, no withdrawals from the scheme occurred.

The society saw several benefits in having external mentors:

- expertise
- minimizing operational impact and indirect costs
- objectivity
- confidentiality
- independence.

The possible limitations were:

- lack of knowledge of the business
- direct costs (which were substantial)
- commitment.

The Model of Mentoring

The programme was designed to last two years and had two purposes:
1. To apply skilled processes, such as visioning, success interviews and personal development plans, to empower an individual to realize innate

potential and to identify and overcome barriers to individual performance.
2. To link realized potential with operational goals to actualize the corporate vision.

However, it is important to say that the process was not psychotherapeutic in nature.

There were four parts to the structure of the mentoring programme:

1. To provide confidential counselling and support.
2. To provide personal management development.
3. To support customer service management—identifying customer and supplier service standards for individual mentees and departments of the society.
4. To ensure that networking and communications provided senior management with information—subject to confidentiality—and an alternative route for communicating upwards issues that could not be resolved by due management process.

The mentoring programme had two phases. Year One concentrated on personal development and support through change and had its focus on the individual. Year Two was more concerned with:

- performance improvement;
- individual, team and committee mentoring;
- team delivery of customer service management sessions to identify the key relationships and standards referred to above.

The programme was completed in December 1992 and created a strategic platform for further initiatives such as coaching with greater line management involvement.

In order to measure the effectiveness of the mentoring programme, the society undertook an ambitious and extremely thorough evaluation and audit of the whole initiative. Considerable resources were dedicated to this task and it is possible within the scope of this study to give some of the key findings.

Evaluation and Learning

The research methodology for data collection comprised:

- a postal questionnaire for all mentees;
- structured interviews with mentees;
- structured interviews with mentors;
- use of a 'core group' of employees whose brief was to become completely *au fait* with the mentoring model itself.

Some of the most interesting responses relate to the relationship itself. As far as meetings were concerned, 59% of the mentees met with their mentors on a weekly basis and 27% fortnightly; 76% of the mentees considered this about right with only around 16% thinking it too frequent. The average length of time in the programme was 18 months. Towards the end of the programme, 45% of mentees thought that the arrangements for ending the relationship could have been improved. Where there was a break in the mentoring relationship—where mentors left the programme—mentees did not always appear to develop as positive a relationship with the new mentor. One of the main learning points from this initiative is that objectives must be made clear at the outset and reinforced during the programme.

Benefits of the Mentoring Programme

The programme was audited every six months in addition to the ongoing evaluation. It was difficult to measure with precision the benefits, as with change management failure is often easier to measure than success. Paradigm shifts affect standards and measurement and it is important to measure the right things. The programme has stimulated individual and collective achievements and the benefits have been most apparent at the individual level. Many of the perceived benefits have come from the counselling and support functions of the mentor.

Benefits to the individual

- 75% of mentees considered that the programme improved their managerial performance by an average of 30%.
- Performance improved, especially in interpersonal, leadership and planning skills.

Other benefits

- Clarity of personal vision.
- Knowledge of barriers to personal performance.
- Knowledge of self and others.
- Improved self-confidence.
- Helping to overcome barriers.
- Improved ability to handle stress.

Benefits to the society

From the audit reports, the following were identified as benefits:

- an improved understanding of vision, mission and objectives;
- people able to identify and overcome barriers to performance;
- improved change management;
- improved management development;
- improved teamwork;
- better leadership.

It is interesting to note that the least successful part of the initiative was the customer service management support sessions, for a variety of reasons to do with objectives and approach. However, both mentors and mentees had a perception that the support sessions were not 'proper mentoring'. This indicates that it is important to know what is appropriate for a mentoring relationship and what the limitations on its use may be.

Some of the benefits of the mentoring initiative expressed as 'personal' viewpoints included:

- helping the 'settling down' process after major reorganization;
- experience of the mentoring process helping to provide a strategic platform for instigating a 'coaching' culture to assist future performance enhancement;
- improved boss–subordinate relationships, becoming more open;
- a more mature management population, producing greater realism;
- a useful 'safety valve' for managers going through major change.

Key Learning from the Mentoring Programme

Factors contributing to its success

1. Regular, permanent one-to-one relationships paced to the needs of the individual.
2. A two-year programme.
3. Quality, integrity and commitment of mentors.
4. Confidentiality.
5. Impartial support and counsel.

What would have improved success

1. Continued demonstrated commitment of top team.
2. Greater clarity and communication of objectives.

3. Feedback on performance of the project.
4. Arrangements for change of mentors.

How to Introduce a Mentoring Programme

- Identify need.
- Have clear objectives which are:
  —well communicated
  —at different levels.
- Obtain continuous demonstrated commitment from top management—it is not enough to say 'we are committed'.
- Structure in flexibility.
- Evaluate continuously using:
  —base data
  —hard and soft data
  —qualitative and quantitative data
  —holistic approach
  —feedback
- Confidentiality and boundaries—establish clear rules and maintain them.
- Brief mentors and mentees.
- Allow at least 18 months for a programme of this type.
- Be clear about the desired values.

This programme has shown that mentoring can support change management and link with other programmes by:

- acting as a safety valve;
- ensuring stability;
- facilitating communication;
- facilitating alignment;
- providing a means of delivering other programmes;
- fulfilling different objectives in different phases of change.

Mentoring can be a means of linking individual managers' development with organizational development by:

- promoting individual and corporate learning;
- encouraging an open and trusting culture;
- facilitating the alignment of individual and corporate vision;
- developing in mentors and mentees the competencies and culture that the organization requires;
- supporting management through change.

The society feels that anyone can benefit from mentoring—individuals, teams and the organization in general at any level.

Challenges for the Programme

- The involvement of line management.
- Ensuring accurate and relevant information flows.
- Ensuring the demonstration of commitment.
- Getting the transition from personal support to 'performance mentoring'.
- Coping with mentors changing.
- Orienting late starters to the programme.

Conclusions

This mentoring programme showed that mentoring is a powerful tool for organizations, particularly in the areas of change management, management and organizational development. It demonstrated that external mentors can be used successfully, that large-scale programmes can work but that continuing demonstrated commitment from top management is vital. However, mentoring is not a panacea and there is no one checklist or prescription. Programmes must be tailored to particular needs, avoid the quick-fix approach and be regarded as a strategic organizational intervention.

COMPANY X

Company X is part of a larger group, a UK financial retailer which has a commercial division, a retail banking and insurance business and also a merchant banking arm. The group employs over 30 000 people, with the majority employed on the retail banking and insurance side of the business. It was a very 'traditional' organization, rather bureaucratic, highly structured, with a strongly controlling culture that was sales driven rather than customer service focused. The pressures of the deregulation of the financial services sector, together with increasing competition in a sophisticated market, form the context for the mentoring initiative.

The aim of the new approach by the organization has been to change in key areas:

- *Service*: from a sales focus—using TQM—to a customer service focus.
- *Structure*: from a bureaucratic, highly structured approach to a process oriented, cross-functional approach.
- *Strategy*: from sophistication to simplicity.
- *Style*: from controlling to coaching and developing.
- *Training and development*: from provider driven to business driven.
- *Learning*: from 'done to you' to self-managed.

Although one of the main thrusts of the change initiative was the desire to move in the direction of self-managed learning, the training and development budget was doubled by senior management to aid the process. One of the foremost challenges to introducing self-managed learning is ensuring that what is learned by an individual is supported in the workplace, so that it is not lost but reinforced and shared. This was felt to be particularly important for senior managers involved in management development programmes. One of the support mechanisms identified as appropriate by the company's management developers was mentoring.

Why does the company encourage mentoring? The reasons can be summarized as to:

- break down barriers;
- influence upwards;
- develop directors as mentors;
- change learning environment;
- manage uncertainty;
- benchmark generic competencies;
- encourage trust and sharing;
- support career development;
- move from management to leadership.

The company has a systematic scheme of management training and development. The programme that we will examine in this context is the Strategic Challenge Programme.

The Strategic Challenge Programme is intended for senior managers with potential to reach director level and above in the organization. It lasts for a 12-month period and comprises five modules with four action learning sets following the launch in January. The mentoring relationship is designed to support the whole process.

Definition of Mentoring

'A process in which one person (mentor) has a responsibility for overseeing the development of another (mentoree) outside the normal manager/subordinate relationship.' The company stresses that mentoring is a relationship, not an activity.

Within the company there were several reasons for introducing mentoring:

- to help inculcate a cross-functional approach to management, therefore using mentoring as an OD strategy;
- to assist managers to break out of the hierarchy, to look up and out of the line relationship;

- as a valid way of helping to develop the directors as mentors;
- to spread learning within the organization;
- to help develop a trusting and sharing culture at the senior levels of the organization;
- to assist in career development and succession planning.

Mentoring was seen in this context as supporting the whole learning strategy by helping mentorees to get to know other parts of the organization, gaining support for project work and for championing the continuity of the programme.

Mentors and Mentorees

The mentorees (nominated for the programme) were at the 'head of' level reporting to directors, who were their mentors. However, they were not in a direct reporting relationship. The mentors were not to be involved in formal appraisal of mentorees at any stage. There was cross-gender mentoring in the scheme which did not pose particular problems. What were the criteria that were used in selecting mentors?

The mentor had to be:

- experienced, with a well-balanced background and successful;
- settled in current position;
- a change agent in personal style and influence;
- accessible, willing and able to invest time;
- patient, with good interpersonal skills;
- committed to developing and nurturing others;
- the possessor of sound and broad knowledge of the company and key objectives;
- capable of an open, trusting relationship.

The Matching Process

The mentors were asked to identify individuals, not in their area of the business, whom they thought that they might be prepared to mentor. This process was replicated for the mentorees. Having taken this information into account, together with people's likes/dislikes, the management developers brought in the line managers to assist in the decision-making process. This helped to get line managers to understand the process and to assist them to 'buy in'. Using several criteria, including location of both parties and sheer 'gut feel', the matching process was completed.

Mentoring Workshops

It was decided to 'train' the mentors in the process and skills which would be required of them. The day event was a combination of the organizational issues and mechanics of the scheme and individual development of interpersonal skills. The event had five main sessions:

- Session 1—Mentoring in context
  —place of mentoring
  —benefits of mentoring.
- Session 2—Place and role of mentor
  —how managers learn
  —learning styles
  —ownership of learning.
- Session 3—Mentoring skills
  —mentor replacement behaviours
  —empathic listening
  —mirroring, pacing, challenging.
- Session 4—Mentoring experience
- Session 5—Practical mentoring in the company

On review, it was felt that mixing these elements of organizational issues and personal skills was not successful, as people at a very senior level do not always feel comfortable with skills activity such as role play. One of the successes of the programme was bringing in mentors from other organizations to talk about their experiences of mentoring.

The mentorees found that their introductory workshop was important. However, one of the problems appeared to be what the mentors were happy talking about in the relationship—one of the terms of the 'contract'. It seems that the mentorees wanted to talk about personal matters and the mentors were more reluctant to do so and preferred to keep the topics in the business area. This was one reason for the skills element being included in the mentors' workshop, to help them cope more with this aspect of the relationship.

Evaluation

The mentors' reactions can be summarized as follows:

- Two-thirds of the relationships worked.
- Up to nine formal meetings took place over the mentoring period.
- Mentors felt it a neutral or good use of their time.
- Benefits to them:
  —more reflective

—new network
—understanding of other parts of the organization.
- Difficulties:
  —developing trusting relationship
  —distance
  —time commitment.

The mentorees' reactions were:

- One-third said that mentoring was a very important part of the programme.
- One-third said that mentoring added value to the programme.
- One-third said that mentoring was totally irrelevant to the programme. However, one of the most important pieces of feedback received from mentorees may have some bearing on this last point: 'Good mentors are interested and show real interest in mentorees.'

Good mentors:

- are open about themselves
- are open about the business
- obtain feedback
- probe
- surprise the mentoree
- make it two way
- are caring
- are human
- are available
- are committed
- are good listeners
- are counsellors.

There were regular review meetings with management developers to monitor the progress of the scheme. It was concluded that only one mentoree should be allocated to a mentor because of time pressures and possible overload of senior executives. It was found that it was best to have the first meeting away from the workplace to facilitate the establishment of the relationship. The mentor should be encouraged to be proactive and not wait for the mentoree to come to them. Some of the effects of the mentoring approach are to stimulate mentorees to become mentors themselves and senior women are coming forward in greater numbers to be mentors.

Within the confines of confidentiality, mentors have been able to identify organizational problems, challenges and opportunities and act on them. They were supporting the non-task element of the programme, in that the projects/tasks were selected by mentorees and line managers as being directly relevant to business needs. This seems to be an essential process in helping to avoid conflict and to stimulate cooperation between line managers and mentors.

The organization concluded that to improve the programme it should do the following:

- Reassess the 'training' day for mentors.
- Prepare the mentorees better in terms of expectations of the relationship.
- Start mentoring later in the programme, giving it more time to 'bed down' at the beginning.
- Have single, not more, mentoring relationships.
- Emphasize:
  —that the first meeting is a social meeting;
  —that objectives and ground rules need to be established at the start;
  —interest and proactivity during crises.

Other benefits to the business have been:

- Managers making connections and opportunities for better integration in learning.
- Building bridges—including cross-functional collaboration/working.
- Stability, realism, stress management.
- Sharing of skills and strategies.
- Challenging/rethinking actions—mentoring refining and improving quality of decision making.
- Relationships more valued—evidence that mentoring has helped to legitimize more collaborative working across functions.

SOME CONCLUSIONS ABOUT MENTORING IN X AND Y

Individuals will take away different ideas and learning from these two examples of mentoring to support change and learning in organizations. One difference between the two approaches is worth investigating, that is the use of mentors who might be deemed to be external to the organization and mentors who are part of the internal management structure. There are advantages and disadvantages to both approaches.

On the whole most organizations will wish to use mentors from within the organization. The reason for this is that much of the benefit of using mentors from within revolves around a deep knowledge and understanding of the organization that is required to perform the role of mentor effectively. This is most obviously true in the case of newly recruited graduates and also high flyers.

The benefit of using external mentors can be seen in the context of Company Y: in terms of support, the participants may have felt able to be more open about their feelings with someone from outside the organization who was therefore perceived as having no axe to grind in the circumstances. There is one important group for whom external mentors are probably a must—chief executives and senior directors. Given the nature of most organizations it will generally be very difficult, if not almost impossible, for a chief executive to have a mentor within their own organization for reasons of politics. Anything said by a chief executive can be misinterpreted and offer unnecessary hostages to fortune. Many chief executives have already built a network of contacts and friends with whom they discuss concerns. However, if it becomes necessary to provide your chief executive with a mentor, the best option may be to look for another experienced chief executive figure rather than someone else trained in listening to people, such as counsellor. Chief executives and directors are often looking for an opportunity to discuss their ideas in a safe environment rather than looking for relief of their angst.

Chapter 9

The Role of Mentoring in Developing Global Managers and Organizations

In the last five to ten years, international corporations have moved up a very steep learning curve in their quest to develop internationally and globally competent managers and organizations. Some companies have been attempting to consolidate and integrate the learning of the past few years.[1]

In some cases, companies are seeking to extend leading-edge human resource practices that have worked well in one country to other countries where they operate. Mentoring is one such practice. One top firm in the electrical engineering industry, for example, has used mentoring successfully in its UK operations. It now wishes to extend mentoring on a pan-European basis and is wondering what it can copy from its UK mentoring activities and what it needs to adapt to local differences.

Other companies are concerned to improve their approaches to developing international managers. In some cases this involves a move away from fragmented, *ad hoc* approaches towards strategic approaches that seek to bring together the different dimensions of developing international managers and to integrate them with business needs. Mentoring is increasingly seen as an important component of this approach. What is the current state of the art in international management development and what role can mentoring play in developing international managers?

A particular type of international manager is coming to prominence. With economic barriers coming down and organizations trying new forms of international coordination, the international manager is becoming someone who can manage across a number of countries and cultures simultaneously. There are two sides to international management competence: international managers need a balanced set of 'doing' and 'being' attributes.

'DOING' COMPETENCIES

The 'doing' competencies are those active, measurable and verifiable (and more changeable) attributes that relate typically to four main roles:

- Championing international strategy
- Operating as cross-border coach and coordinator
- Acting as intercultural mediator and change agent
- Managing personal effectiveness for international business.

As a champion of international strategy, the international manager collaborates with managers and other employees from other countries to envision the future and formulate international strategies to take the organization forward. The manager also increasingly needs to understand business processes and the way that these cut across organizational and geographical boundaries. As cross-border coach, the international manager increasingly works with individuals and local management teams in a way that emphasizes collaboration as equals, providing ideas and support, encouraging their people to contribute and develop their own ideas, and seeking opportunities to develop them through the job. More and more managers need to develop the process facilitation skills required to manage teams whose members are culturally mixed and geographically dispersed.

Creating flexible yet cohesive international organizations involves considerable change and demands new ways of thinking and working. As international mediators and change agents, international managers need to be able to switch their frame of reference rapidly between different cultures and drive in different gears, rather than just one gear. They must be aware of their own cultural underpinnings and of the need to be sensitive to cultural differences. But they must also be able to manage change in different cultural contexts and this means testing the boundaries of those cultures. International managers have to appreciate why different cultures do things differently, but they must not let themselves be paralysed by such differences or accept cultural excuses for inaction. On the other hand, they must not assume that approaches to change that work successfully in one culture will work effectively in another. One of the biggest problems for the international manager is to dig below surface explanations to understand what is really happening locally. Some managers try to address this problem by cultivating a 'culture guide', perhaps a respected senior manager in the local unit, who can help them interpret the situation and also give them feedback on their personal impact locally.

A further critical competency is the individual's ability to manage their effectiveness for international business. The international manager's job involves a great deal of travelling and a lot of stress. The average manager spends about 120 days, or a third of a year, away from their home base—and many managers spend substantially more time than this working abroad. This makes it very difficult for them to achieve a satisfactory balance between work and private life and the costs imposed on the family can be considerable. Many international managers admit that they do not manage this aspect of their lives very well.

The exact nature of the 'doing' competencies is likely to vary according to the type of organization. Indeed, one of the features of the current international management development scene is the diversity of types of company now interested in developing international competencies. No longer is international management development the concern only of big multinational companies. It is now of interest to a large number of diverse organizations. These include, for example, fast-growing mid-sized companies, rapidly internationalizing service businesses, and some of the cross-border strategic alliances and long-term partnerships that have been created in the last few years. Each of these types of company will have their own particular needs for international management development. Whatever the differences at the 'doing' level, however, there are some fundamental attributes that will probably be needed by all international managers regardless of the type of organization in which they operate.

'BEING' COMPETENCIES

The success of effective international managers is not solely due to specific behavioural skills. It seems that many successful international managers are operating from a deeper, more enduring core competency that is essentially holistic. It is clear that the job of the international manager is very challenging and makes heavy demands on both the individual and the family. But successful international managers have developed a philosophy of life or 'being' that enables them to meet those challenges and demands. This other side or 'being' underpins and sustains the active side of the job. It concerns the way that such people think and feel and the beliefs and values that motivate them.

A central component here is a facility for 'complex thinking': the ability to see several dimensions in a situation rather than only one dimension, and to consider several solutions rather than only one solution. This is an attribute that helps the manager to put aside habitual ways of thinking and to start to get into the heads of people who think differently from them. It depends critically on active listening and on a sense of humility that allows people to admit that they do not know everything and to seek help from others where necessary. People with this capacity tend to search for diverse information, not only information that confirms their previous conclusions.

The deeper, psychological side also involves an emotional resilience that allows the individual to take interpersonal risks and deal with personally uncomfortable or stressful situations. It includes values such as a strong curiosity to learn that often stays vibrant throughout the individual's career.

'BECOMING' INTERNATIONAL

Because of the need for continuous adaptation and learning, the international manager also needs the additional attribute of 'becoming'. This is a mindset that implies that the individual is open to continuous learning and thus develops maturity and wisdom combined with modesty and openness. Many successful managers have to learn from painful early mistakes in their international career and therefore recognize their need to learn from others, no matter how senior they become, as they move through new international environments.

From an organizational perspective, companies need to adopt more integrated approaches to international management development. There are some important issues to consider in designing appropriate approaches: first, the need for a long-term view; and secondly, the need to build in support for learning.

A Long-Term View

The kinds of competencies summarized here, especially the all-important 'being' qualities, are not developed overnight. Taking a longer-term view and a more systematic approach to developing the potential of international managers does not imply imposing a cumbersome and rigid process on organizations. Maintaining flexibility and taking advantage of opportunities as they arise are essential in developing these managers. Learning opportunities are used more effectively when they are embedded in a developmental perspective.

Support for Learning

Whatever the development approaches adopted, it is important for a key element in the individual's learning process to receive more attention: the need for reflection in order to understand an experience, draw out the learning and assimilate it in new behaviour and thinking. Neglect of this aspect often hampers managers in their ability to learn from experiences on the job. They do not have the time or opportunity to extract the learning from an experience because they are constantly moving on from one activity to the next. A key challenge for management development, therefore, is to build opportunities for reflection into the work of managers, as well as creating new activities for them to experience. The opportunity to reflect in dialogue is particularly valuable, whether it be through discussions with peers, coaches, mentors or other learning partners, because they allow the manager to explore different interpretations of events and behaviours. Mentoring is now being explicitly used in a number of European firms to develop international capabilities.

How are the qualities described here to be fostered and developed in international managers? We suggest that 'doing' and 'being' are combined in a career-long process of 'becoming international' in which there are some critical moments in an individual's development where there is very high potential for transition in their 'being' —in effect, an experience after which the world never looks the same as it did before. These may include a new job (in particular, an international assignment), a secondment, membership of an international project team, or participation in a management programme.

INTERNATIONAL ASSIGNMENTS AS LEARNING EXPERIENCES

International assignments are potentially one of the most powerful means of developing international competence. Company thinking about international assignments differs. One meets both companies which intend to expand the opportunities for their people to undertake such assignments and those which are trying to reduce the amount of expatriation, largely to reduce costs. In either case, it is important to exploit the learning and development potential of whatever international assignments are undertaken by individuals, and to do it more effectively than most organizations have done in the past. As one manager interviewed during the Ashridge research said:

We as a company do a very poor job of preparing people for an international experience. We take people and throw them into the deep end of the pool. We get some Olympic champions out of that but we drown some good people too. We could get so much more return on our investment in international assignments if we supported their learning and development.

Managers on international assignments need to think about three levels of learning (see Figure 9.1).

Assignment-Related Learning

The question that the manager should ask here is: What do I need to learn that will help me perform effectively in *this* international assignment? This is learning for the 'now' and, where companies or individuals give any thought to learning, this is probably the area on which they concentrate. In an expatriate context, this may well include such obvious areas as language or cultural awareness training. Where it takes place at all in companies, it is likely to occur before or during the early stages of the assignment. As already noted, some successful international managers have learned the value of identifying and

Figure 9.1

What do I need to learn that will help me perform effectively in *this* international assignment? → ASSIGNMENT-RELATED LEARNING

ORGANIZATIONAL LEARNING

How do I help the organization as a whole to learn internationally?

LEARNING FOR THE FUTURE

What am I learning that will:
— help me to carry out my next (international) job effectively?
— equip me to manage in an international company in future?

Figure 9.1 Learning Through International Assignments

working with a local 'culture guide' to help them with ongoing learning about the local situation during the assignment.

Learning for the Future

The question here is: What am I learning that will (a) help me to carry out my next job effectively (especially if it is another international posting), and (b) equip me to manage in an international company in future? This requires individuals to lift their heads above the challenges of the current job and to reflect about their future direction. It also means staying in touch with developments in the wider organization to understand organizational and management trends.

Organizational Learning

Critical questions here are: How do I help the organization as a whole to learn internationally? What is the one most important thing that will change or that the organization will do differently as a result of my having carried out this assignment? It is frequently asserted today that one of the keys to competing in a fast-moving and increasingly complex global business environment will be a capacity for organizational learning. The manager working on assignment in another country should be particularly well placed to contribute to this process. Again, this demands the ability to see and understand how one's contribution and ideas fit into the big picture, something that is not always easy when working away from the corporate centre.

It is natural that, before and in the early stages of an international posting, assignment-related learning will loom large and be the dominant source of concern for the individual. As the assignment proceeds, however, one would expect the other two dimensions of learning to become increasingly important. Day-to-day business may prevent the assignee from giving such wider questions due attention.

Whether or not such learning takes place or whether the earlier described transition in 'being' takes place during an international assignment may depend on the way that the experience is facilitated. A key element in the learning process, as described by Kolb (1984), is often missing in the work and development experiences of managers: the need for reflection in order to understand and make better sense of an experience, draw out the learning and assimilate it in new behaviour. Successful international managers do not consign what others consider to be mere everyday episodes to the wastepaper basket. Instead, they reflect on them and glean as many lessons from them as possible. Mentors can play a powerful role in supporting this learning.

USING MENTORING TO DEVELOP INTERNATIONAL MANAGERS

Organizations are particularly interested in the use of mentoring in the management development process in general. We believe that mentoring can be a particularly powerful approach in the international sphere. For those organizations that regard international mobility as a strategic necessity, mentoring can help to ease the process. For example, management developers have commented that it can be a particular challenge to move South East Asian managers out of their 'home' countries. This can sometimes circumscribe the competitiveness of the organization, as it cannot use the skills of these people in critical markets, and also impinges on the development of the individuals themselves. These companies believe that mentoring and the support that it provides for the individual on assignment abroad have the potential to overcome the barriers that impede mobility. Also, the support and link with the home base provided by the mentor can prevent expatriate failure and the premature return of the assignee, with all its associated costs for the individual and the organization. Some companies believe that international mentoring is not just preventive but can go further to produce positive benefits. A Swiss company says that it provides its international trainees with mentors to achieve 'a more impactful assignment'. Let us examine how mentoring can positively enhance international assignments.

We have already noted the way in which some international managers seek the help of 'culture guides' when working in new countries. They might apply this strategy to help them learn and reflect on a wider plane about their work. In particular, the different kinds of learning described above that should take place during an international assignment might be powerfully supported by providing the assignee with a mentor, outside of the individual's reporting line, elsewhere in the organization. The role of the mentor would be to provide the support, counselling and *challenge* necessary to facilitate the individual's learning. This role encompasses acting as an 'eye opener' and as a sounding board for ideas. An internationally experienced mentor can provide an understanding of how the organization works in different countries, of how and why decisions are taken and with what effect. A mentor who has a track record of managing international teams and operations can also provide a role model for the mentoree to emulate or against which to benchmark their own behaviour.

Where assignment-related learning for the current job is concerned, internationally experienced mentors can draw on their own experience to provide some general principles about operating in an unfamiliar environment. If they have experience of the country and culture in which the assignee is operating, they might themselves act as a culture guide or supplement the advice given by the local guide. As international management researcher Ariane Berthoin Antal (1993) says, to fulfil their international responsibilities: 'managers need to understand the people they are dealing with, and to have a feeling for different ways of approaching problems and making decisions that are embedded in the traditions of each culture'. While some of the information can be communicated through special training programmes, much is informal knowledge that is best passed on from individual to individual. Faced with an unknown situation, a manager needs to have someone to turn to for help in interpreting what is going on and for advice on how to proceed. Only a person who really knows the culture in question can provide this kind of support. International mentoring can provide the framework for developing the necessary trusting and open relationship in which a manager can discuss the entire range of issues with which they need to grapple, both at the office and outside it.

It is in the other two domains of learning—future and organizational—that a mentor outside the country in question may have a particularly special role to play. The role of the mentor here is to help the individual keep the big picture in mind and to stay in touch with developments in the company and business environment at large. One company, General Electric of the US, talks of the need to develop 'global brains' in its managers—giving them an understanding of world competition and what it takes to match and beat it by opening their eyes to 'a wider and faster playing field'. The international mentor with their view of the big picture can play a critical role in developing such global understanding. The mentor can also encourage the individual to think regularly about how they will feed back learning from the assignment to the wider organization, both during the assignment and after it. The mentors with their wide range of contacts in the organization can serve as a useful conduit for global learning.

International assignments do not only involve managers going abroad from the corporate centre. Some companies bring managers from their overseas operations to head office for a tour of duty as part of their development. Mentoring can help non-parent company managers working on assignment at the corporate centre to understand the culture of the parent organization and what it takes to get on in the organization.

We have indicated that mentoring has the power to replicate itself in organizations. That is to say that people who have had mentors and have benefited from the relationship are often enthusiastic about acting as mentors for others. In the international context, this means that people who have had mentors while on international assignments and experienced the relationship working (especially coping with time and distance) might themselves make excellent mentors.

There is one other tendency in organizations that has a bearing on the way in which international managers learn and develop: the trend to self-development. This is significant for managers for two reasons. First, even more companies are shifting their human resource policy from one of mechanistically assigning staff to courses to one of assigning responsibility for development to the staff themselves, while providing guidance and support. Mentoring can be an important component of the support provided here.

Secondly, the speed with which change is occurring in and around organizations operating internationally makes life-long learning, as already noted, a crucial factor in individual and corporate success. This implies that initiative (for example, in seeking out a mentor) and self-knowledge (which a mentor can encourage) are key competencies that managers must nurture throughout their careers, especially in an international context.

Earlier research in international management development identified some pioneering companies who were already integrating mentors into their international management development processes (Barham and Devine, 1991). Expatriates at the French pharmaceutical firm Rhône–Poulenc used to be assigned 'godfathers', someone with whom they could keep in regular contact and who helped them consider and negotiate their next career step. The godfather was usually a senior manager with wide relationships with other managers across the group. This meant that they did not have a compartmentalized perspective but could alert their mentorees to a variety of different career opportunities. International Distillers & Vintners appointed senior managers as 'godparents' to stay in touch with the development of the international assignees in its International Management Cadre Programme.

Mentoring is a well-established practice in many US firms and some have extended its use to the international arena. AT&T and Colgate-Palmolive have used mentors to keep in touch with expatriates' progress abroad, to update them on news at head office and to act as troubleshooters for them and HQ departments. Another US firm, Philip Morris, looks for mentors who are expatriates themselves, believing that having been there makes them particularly valuable resources.

Other companies are now following these examples. International mentoring may be introduced in one part of an organization before being applied more widely. The manufacturing operations of UK pharmaceuticals conglomerate Glaxo Wellcome have introduced a programme to provide joint sponsors/mentors for people taking international assignments. One person from the host country and one from the home country help to ensure continuity for people going abroad to work. Glaxo Wellcome's senior HR managers see this as an example of excellent people development practice that it would like to extend to other parts of the company.

Scandinavian Airlines System (SAS) uses mentoring to link managers in key overseas posts to 'create the conditions for the mentorees to consolidate the network at home' and to support the re-entry process. The company believes that people abroad can feel 'lost' and therefore need to have someone at home who cares about them and with whom they can get in touch. SAS recognizes that distance is an important issue in international mentoring as it constrains the amount of face-to-face communication that mentors and mentorees are able to achieve. One of the important questions which the company is investigating about 'distance mentoring' concerns what distinguishes the people who can make the mentoring relationship work despite the problems of distance, as opposed to those who have difficulties in coping with distance. SAS also suggests that distance means that more time than the typical one-year timespan of 'domestic' mentoring may be needed to make an international mentoring relationship work. SAS emphasizes that it is always the needs of the individual mentoree that are the main consideration in mentoring, whether the mentoree is international or in the home organization. This also makes it possible for the mentoree to choose the most appropriate mentor.

The UK telecommunications company Cable & Wireless is an organization which believes that mentoring can support the international mobility which is regarded as a strategic fundamental for the business. In this federation of companies encompassing 60 000 employees in 50 countries, mobility is important for three reasons: to deploy people rapidly in new business developments around the world; to give key managers experience in an international marketplace; and to transfer skills and knowledge across the group. The growing importance of the latter means that the company no longer looks only to the UK for expertise but tries to draw on its worldwide pool of employees.

The company has set up an international resourcing and development unit to provide support services to the group. This is a shared service unit that is funded by the federation of businesses that use it. It therefore has to be cost effective and to offer a comprehensive service because it competes with outside suppliers. This means developing marketing, negotiating and selling skills not traditionally associated with a human resource function. It is responsible for ensuring that the best people are considered for the job, that they are properly briefed and trained for the assignment, and that their families receive support in making the move. It arranges remuneration, benefits and all aspects of the relocation process. It also sponsors a number of international development programmes that examine local management style and corporate culture.

The unit has also established international career action centres to provide a range of career counselling services for all employees, which has been particularly successful for people on international assignment. These centres enable people to talk in confidence about their careers, both within their department and internationally. They are also a means of tackling the problem of re-entry. Six months before the individuals return to their home base, they are contacted by the centre, sent an information pack, given information about what is happening in the group as a whole and advice on how to manage the re-entry process, including writing résumés and personal marketing techniques. If they do not have a job on return, they have one-to-one coaching to help them find another job within the group.

Cable & Wireless views mentoring as an approach which links with the work of its career action centres, particularly in keeping in touch with individual expatriates and their development needs and aspirations. Cable & Wireless is also now relying less on career expatriates. It sees mentoring as one way of making up for the loss of the traditional network of expatriate managers which acted as a support for international assignees in the past. Mentoring is also seen as useful in overcoming the lack of understanding and limited or narrow horizons that can exist in the expatriate's home unit, which may prevent people there from seeing the value of overseas experience. It is regarded as a valuable learning opportunity for the mentor as they get to know what it is like working in an overseas business and about the issues involved.

Such cases show that the mentor, with their close knowledge of the individual and the wider organization, can play a useful role in easing the re-entry process when an assignment finishes. The problems that returning expatriates frequently experience during the re-entry phase at the end of their assignments are by now well documented (Adler, 1991). Giving more attention to the future and organizational dimensions of learning in a mentoring process would go a long way towards easing the frequent complaint of returning expatriates that, when they returned to home base, nobody ever asked them about what had happened or what they had learned.

It is not only large multinational companies who can benefit from international mentoring. Globalization means that more and more small and medium-sized businesses need to develop international or global capability. They have fewer fixed attitudes about international management development and may be open to new approaches. One such firm is Nordson Corporation, an industrial paint and sealant equipment manufacturer based in Ohio, US. Nordson went international by following its US customers abroad and now derives 60% of its turnover from abroad. It has 15 'inpatriates' in the US from Europe, Asia, Latin America and Africa. These include new hires, intra-company transferees on multi-year assignments and transferees serving for less than one year. The company appoints a domestic mentor to help each inpatriate integrate into the US business culture and to learn how to be effective on the job. Using mentoring to integrate managers from abroad into the parent culture is a strategy that large companies can use to advantage (Ioannou, 1995).

Expatriates (and inpatriates) have always faced the problems of feeling isolated or exposed in working in different cultures. These difficulties are now compounded by the advent of the flatter, leaner organization in which more and more managers are working without the traditional line reporting structures. Mentoring not only aids development but also helps individuals to feel that they are not working in isolation.

COPING WITH TIME AND DISTANCE

Many companies have indicated that managers have problems making time available for mentoring, though evaluations have shown that it is often the busiest managers who are the most creative in using their time effectively. How can individuals and their mentors develop effective relationships when working at a possibly considerable geographical distance from each other? In a domestic setting, there are more opportunities for mentors and mentorees to meet. Organizations will need to be prepared to spend resources to bring people together, at least at the begining of a mentoring scheme. Only if international mentoring is positioned as a strategic intervention will organizations commit the necessary resources.

How often mentor and mentoree meet depends on individual circumstances, travel budgets and whether the participants can build meetings into their travel schedules. Some international assignees return to home base at regular intervals and this is an obvious time for them to meet with their mentors. Attention needs to be given to how people will communicate between face-to-face meetings. One UK-based mentor who has a mentoree in Africa points to the need for much more careful planning of when and how to contact each other. Time constraints during telephone calls, for example, may mean that in extra preparation each participant sends the other a list of topics that they would like to cover. This also gives each participant time to think about their responses and maximizes the impact of the mentoring relationship.

The new communication and networking technologies promise to assist the mentoring process here. According to consultant Eddie Obeng of Pentacle The Virtual Business School, 'there is a growing need for local learning—learning which is continuously adapted and fitted around the immediate needs of managers. If access to learning is immediate, it becomes a far more valuable managerial currency' (Crainer, 1995). Pentacle is using technology to mentor managers in client companies. 'The constant interaction allowed by networking on the information superhighway turns mentoring into a far more dynamic, customer-focused and practical exercise,' says Obeng. Although the definition of mentoring here seems to be closer to coaching for the immediate job, the potential for IT to support learning relationships is clear.

The new technology means that people are no longer limited to finding a mentor within their own company. 'Cast an electronic net,' says one commentator, 'and chances are you'll find advisors who share your professional concerns and challenges' (*Training and Development*, 1994). More and more people post messages on on-line bulletin boards and in-house e-mail systems to find experienced colleagues who are willing to offer career advice and support. Through the Internet, it is increasingly possible to find and communicate with such unofficial mentors around the globe. One of the most difficult issues that the busy international manager faces (whether as an expatriate or a frequent traveller) is managing the balance between work and private life. It may be that mentors could play a valuable role in advising individuals to help them keep a sense of proportion on this aspect of their lives.

AN INTERNATIONAL MENTOREE

This person is a young project manager working in an international business unit of Ericsson, a Swedish telecommunications company. She joined a mentoring programme that the company originally introduced for female managers in Sweden. Because she knew that she would soon be taking up an international assignment in Germany, she sought a mentor with expatriate experience who could advise her on cultural adaptation and about doing business in Germany. A senior manager with considerable international experience (now the chief executive of her unit) was appointed as her mentor. He advised her: 'Speak the language. Be tough. Keep on asking questions.'

Her first boss in Germany was a Swede but part-way through her assignment, a local German manager became her boss. She encountered difficulties with her new boss partly, she felt, because he did not appreciate her proactive style in meetings and because he did not consider it legitimate for a woman to pursue a career in management, especially when she announced that she was getting married.

The mentee would have liked to seek the counsel of her mentor in Sweden but the lack of opportunity to meet him face to face together with her inhibitions about bothering a very busy senior manager on the telephone limited this as a source of help. Rather disillusioned, she planned her return to Sweden and was able to gain the support of her mentor in finding a new role there. She was now working with her mentor to put what had been a painful experience for her in perspective and to get back on track with her career.

THE INTERNATIONAL MENTOR

The individual mentoree has much to gain from the mentoring relationship. What is in it for the mentor? International mentors not only gain personal satisfaction from helping the development of an individual, but also have the chance to deepen their own international understanding and to take the pulse of the company's international operations.

Ariane Berthoin Antal (1993) suggests that 'the benefits to a mentor may be even greater in international mentoring than in monocultural relationships. The mentor who serves as a role model and coach for behaviour in his or her culture automatically receives insights and coaching as regards behaviour and thinking in the culture of the mentee. The cultural stimulation and learning opportunity for a senior manager in this situation is rare.'

Through their experience, international mentors should have developed strong cross-cultural awareness—an understanding that the thinking and behaviour of people and organizations in different countries are influenced by different and deeply-embedded asssumptions about the world. They understand that things cannot always be expected to work the same way in other countries as they do at home. They should also ideally be effective international networkers inside and outside the organization, so that they can introduce their mentorees to other people in different countries who can also assist in development.

In particular, if we are trying to develop successful international managers with such characteristics as complex thinking and a curiosity to learn, we hope that mentorees would be able to find such qualities in their mentors. The latter need to be able to help their mentorees think through sometimes difficult or sensitive situations in different cultural contexts, to consider different dimensions in those situations and to generate different options. They need to encourage their mentorees not to 'close down' their thinking too early on a given situation. To do this, the mentors must allow themselves to have an open learning style. They must have the continuing curiosity to learn that allows them to see that they can also learn from the mentoring experience. In our workshops, we sometimes ask participants to describe the 'mentor from hell' as a way of identifying the qualities that would disqualify managers from acting as mentors. For us, the 'international mentor from hell' is a culturally insensitive senior manager who thinks that they have learned it all.

Attributes of the International Mentor

- Coaching and counselling skills.
- Internationally experienced (including living and working abroad if mentoring an international assignee).

- Keen understanding of international imperatives and challenges faced by the organization and its global strategies.
- Cross-cultural awareness.
- International networker inside and outside the organization.
- Complex thinker, open learning style, continuing curiosity to learn.
- Sees mentoring as an opportunity and an investment for themselves and the organization, not a cost.

MENTORING AS INTERNATIONAL ORGANIZATIONAL DEVELOPMENT

We have looked at using mentoring to support individuals working away from their home base. However, we have already noted the role that mentors can play in capturing organizational learning from international assignments. The organization as a whole can benefit in other ways from international mentoring approaches. For example, they can be used to develop a global perspective among emergent international managers or younger high potentials. This can involve giving such future international managers mentors in other countries (and perhaps other functions).

It might also involve providing managers in overseas subsidiaries with mentors at the corporate centre to help them learn about the parent organization and its global objectives. Such an initiative can include an explicit international organizational development objective whereby it not only contributes to the development of international perspectives and a strong personal network for the individual, but also simultaneously fosters the development of wider organizational networks and synergistic links.

Such networks and links foster the timely sharing of ideas and expertise so essential for organizational learning in the fast-changing global business environment of the future. International mentoring relationships between different parts of a company can lay the groundwork for building networks that span continents and cultures. They can improve communication across boundaries and provide a channel for new ideas and innovation to flow between countries. Workshops that bring together mentors and mentorees for training and debriefing also contribute to the formation of international networks and to the development of the international company's 'organizational glue'. As one of the aims of mentoring in this context is to create the international organization, it cannot be expected that the organization will be able to find in all its subsidiaries mentors with wide international experience. Whatever their background, however, the open learning qualities described above will be essential if cross-border exchange is to work. ABB, the Swedish–Swiss global power engineering group, says that its managers need to be 'givers not takers' and this is very much the sort of mindset on which international mentoring will depend.

There may be other organizational benefits from an international mentoring scheme. For example, by showing a long-term commitment by the corporate centre to the development of people in the different countries in which the organization operates, international mentoring also has the potential to improve morale and motivation across the organization's global activities.

One company that is looking to mentoring as a route to international organizational development is Stora, a Swedish forest industries company. Stora believes that mentoring can help it build a global organization. It is using mentoring to underpin the development of global capabilities from an early stage in the careers of its managers and simultaneously to bring about the change of culture and mindset required by a global corporation. It is introducing a mentorship scheme to encourage international integration and synergy across the organization and to support leadership for young managers in their first managerial position. As one aim of the scheme is to promote mobility between different parts of the business, the 'adepts' or mentorees are paired with mentors from different business areas, giving the mentoree access to experience and understanding of how to gain promotion in another area of the business.

To stimulate a global perspective and a wider understanding of the business, mentorees are deliberately linked with mentors from different countries, cultures and functional backgrounds. As Stora believes that cultural differences can affect the mentoring programme, mentors must have experience in the same culture in which the adept is working. They must be senior people with an interest in other people's development, have a successful track record and be seen as a good leadership model. Stora believes that mentoring offers internationally experienced senior managers who act as mentors the chance to share and to be valued for their international experience.

Stora is paying careful attention to the mentoring process. The one-year programme starts with a two-day seminar where mentors and adepts start the mentoring process. Mentors are given training in the mentoring role (in particular, in how to share experiences without 'taking over') and adepts start formulating goals for their area of responsibility and for their career. To provide context, Stora senior managers present the company's visions for the future and the Stora human resources concept. Thereafter, mentors and adepts will maintain regular contact and it is the adept's responsibility to manage these contacts. It is envisaged that some of the contacts can be in personal meetings but that much can be done by telephone. The quality and frequency are seen as more important than personal meetings *per se*. The adepts will start work on their PPD (Planning Personal Development) in which they focus on their individual strengths and weaknesses and set their future career goals.

Three to four months after the first seminar, mentors and adepts join together in a seminar focusing on leadership and leadership styles. In this seminar, the aim is that they together develop a mutual understanding of global leadership through a computer-based leadership simulator. In the simulator they manage and lead a company over a simulated timespan of four years. This second seminar ends with the production of a plan for future cooperation between mentor and adept. Afterwards, regular contacts will continue as before but with a shared experience of ideas about leadership from the simulation exercise. A last seminar at the end of the year rounds up the process. In this final seminar, questions of high priority for Stora are presented and discussed and leadership issues are addressed. The mentoring experience is also evaluated for both the adepts and the mentors. The mentoring programme was still in its pilot stage at Stora at the time of writing, but the company's senior HR staff were very excited about its prospects.

INTERNATIONAL MENTORING: OPPORTUNITIES, BENEFITS AND ISSUES

International mentoring is still a relatively new activity for many companies, but some general opportunities and benefits can be deduced from their experience so far. For the organization, these are as follows:

- Enhanced business performance across borders.
- Helping international assignments to achieve real impact.

- Improved international communication, including global strategy.
- Reduced rates of expatriate failure.
- Better integration across borders.
- Capturing and facilitating of global organizational learning.
- Greater cross-cultural understanding between the different parts of the company.
- Improvement of international management competencies among key managers.

For the individual, the opportunities and benefits are:

- Support during international assignments in terms of:
  —link to the organization and the 'big picture';
  —maintaining motivation;
  —cross-cultural guidance;
  —enhanced learning;
  —facilitating re-entry.
- Support in meeting business objectives and making an impact.
- Enhancing career vision.
- Developing international management competencies, including cross-cultural competencies and 'global brains'.
- Support for the individual during international change processes.
- Opportunity for the mentor to share and be valued for their international experience.
- Help for non-parent country managers in understanding what is needed to progress in the organization.

While international mentoring offers some important opportunities and benefits, it complicates three issues in particular. These are the 'tyrannies' of time, distance and culture. Time involves not only the problems of communicating across different time zones—that is a fact of life in a global company. However, if mentoring is done 'out of hours', as much is, in an international situation it may place almost intolerable burdens on both participants unless managed imaginatively. Lack of time, exacerbated in the international context, can prove a real challenge to introducing effective mentoring schemes. True commitment is needed on all sides.

New communications media offer opportunities for mentors and mentorees to stay in touch across geographical distances, but psychological barriers remain (such as inhibition by a more junior manager about contacting a busy senior manager with what may be thought by the mentoree to be a relatively trivial matter). Such issues need to be surfaced at the beginning of the relationship to legitimize how and when mentors and mentorees will contact each other. Time and distance mean more planning in mentoring in the international context.

Culture remains. What is the impact of culture on the dynamics of mentoring and how will it operate in different cultural settings? We explore this in the next chapter.

INTERNATIONAL MENTORING SELF-ASSESSMENT

- What is the purpose of international assignments in your organization?
  —Fulfilment of immediate business need?
  —Career development?
  —Organizational development?
  —Or all three?
- How can mentoring support these objectives?
- Is it important for your people to develop international or global perspectives? How can mentoring add value in this area?
- Do you have people capable of being international mentors and commited?

SUMMARY OF KEY LEARNING

- Companies are moving away from fragmented appproaches to international management development towards strategic approaches that bring together the different dimensions of developing international managers and integrate them with business needs. Mentoring is seen increasingly as an important component of this approach.
- Developing international managers requires that they are given support for learning, encouragement and opportunity to reflect on their experience.
- Mentoring can support people undertaking international assignments by making these more effective learning experiences. Mentors can help expatriates to understand the business culture of

the parent company. The role of mentor is to provide support, advice and challenge for the individual assignee in thinking through the learning needed for the immediate assignment, learning for the future and how to contribute to organizational learning.
- Time and distance in international mentoring require mentors and mentorees to plan their interactions more carefully. International mentoring relationships may take more time to be effective.
- The international mentor needs to be culturally sensitive and to have an open learning style.
- Mentoring across borders can be used to develop the international organization by creating global perspectives among young high potentials, by fostering networks and by encouraging synergy between the different parts of the organization.

Endnote
[1]This chapter builds on two conference papers: (1) 'Developing International Management Competencies', presented by Kevin Barham to the European Institute for Advanced Studies in Management (EIASM) 2nd European Conference on International Staffing and Expatriate Management, Braga, Portugal, June 26–27, 1995; (2) 'Integrating Approaches to International Management Development', presented by Kevin Barham to the International Consortium for Executive Development Research (ICEDR) Forum on Developing Global Capability, Darden School of Management, University of Virginia, 20–23 May 1996.

Chapter 10

The Impact of Cultural Differences on International Mentoring

The management of expectations is the key to the successful application of mentoring. One of the factors with the biggest impact on expectations in the international sphere is culture. Advocates of mentoring will often claim that the approach can offer benefits in any cultural context. While we sympathize with that view, there is by now plenty of research evidence which implies that the cultural dimension is an important issue for mentoring and other human resource policies. Whether companies are using mentoring to develop international managers or planning to introduce mentoring into their human resource development activities in the countries where they operate, they have not only to consider the technical aspects of designing a mentoring scheme but also devise a process that takes the *potential* impact of cultural differences into account.

What, for example, might happen when a senior German manager acts as mentor to a younger French manager? What are the implications of introducing a successful mentoring process designed in the UK into the Italian subsidiary of your company?

CULTURAL DIFFERENCES AND ORGANIZATIONAL BEHAVIOUR

That cultural differences can have a significant effect on organizational behaviour and management and leadership styles in different countries has been shown by a number of important studies. To quote just two influential studies:

Culture is the collective programming of the mind which distinguishes the members of one group or category of people from another. . . . One should think twice before applying the norms of one person, group or society to another. Information about the nature of the cultural differences between societies, their roots, and their consequences should precede judgement and action. (Hofstede, 1991)

Culture is the way in which a group of people solves problems. . . . Every culture distinguishes itself from others by the specific solutions it chooses to certain problems. . . . Culture is like gravity: you do not experience it until you jump six feet into the air. Local managers may not openly criticize a centrally developed appraisal system or reject the matrix organization, especially if confrontation or defiance is not culturally acceptable to them. In practice, though, beneath the surface, the silent forces of culture operate a destructive process, biting at the roots of centrally-developed methods which do not 'fit' locally. (Trompenaars, 1993)

In this chapter we aim to consider information about cultural differences and their possible consequences for mentoring approaches in different societies. Our aim is to provide a culturally robust framework for thinking about the way that mentoring might work in different cultural contexts. To create such a framework, we draw on some of the leading models of cultural differences to identify those dimensions of cultural difference that might be expected to affect mentoring. We suggest some issues that might arise and some questions that need to be asked about the way in which each cultural dimension might impinge on mentoring, whether favourably or unfavourably.

Individuals and organizations, of course, vary widely within cultures and may be more or less 'committed' to the prevailing cultural norms. There are also different levels of culture in addition to those at the national level, including corporate, functional and professional cultures. The framework here is not meant to be used in a deterministic way but rather as a stimulus to thinking through some of the factors that need to be taken into account when planning and implementing mentoring in different cultural settings. What are the questions that you need to ask to be aware of possible difficulties—and also conceivable advantages on which to build a mentoring initiative?

Research shows that the behaviour we see in different cultures is only the tip of the iceberg (a number of cross-cultural researchers, including André Laurent and Ariane Berthoin Antal, have used the analogy of the iceberg to describe the influence of culture on society). Underneath lie the values, norms and deeply held and often unconscious assumptions that affect behaviour. As one international manager, himself a mentor to a young manager, says: 'We all speak the same words but we have different agendas.' A representative of an international company who took part in one of our workshops described how one of his firm's overseas subsidiaries paid lip service to corporate goals about empowering its employees but still continued to operate in practice as a very hierarchical organization: 'These things go very deep. Culture does not change overnight.'

'The dimensions of cultural difference that might be expected to affect mentoring range from its impact at a macro or organizational level to its impact on mentoring processes and relationships and on individuals involved in mentoring. These 'iceberg factors' include:

- Change (low versus high uncertainty avoidance)
- Power (high versus low centralization)
- Communication flow (acceptability outside the hierarchy)
- Group (versus individual)
- Status (who you are versus what you do)
- Ego (high versus low tendency)
- Leadership (manager as expert versus facilitator)
- Communication context (high versus low)
- Involvement (high versus low).

The different aspects of mentoring against which the cultural dimensions are ranged include:

- Legitimacy of mentoring
- The mentoring agreement
- The mentor
- The mentoring relationship
- The mentoree
- Feedback style
- The line manager
- Confidentiality.

Setting the different iceberg factors or cultural dimensions against the different aspects of mentoring, as in Figure 10.1, provides us with a framework for thinking about the way that mentoring might work. It enables us to consider some of the issues and expectations we need to consider when setting up a mentoring initiative abroad. As such, it is not a pigeon hole for definitive answers but a springboard for questions. The iceberg factors in Figure 10.1 range from those on the left which impact at the organizational level (change, power etc.) to those on the right which can affect individual relationships (communication context, involvement etc.).

As a further guide, we have drawn on existing cross-cultural research to give an indication of how different countries potentially rank against the different dimensions of culture in terms of a high, medium or low propensity to each. These rankings are *indicative* only.

It may be that where a country ranks as medium against a certain dimension (as opposed to high or low), one needs to give even more thought to possible consequences. The highs and lows may be easier to address than the medium scores because the latter are less clear. While most of the major economies are included in the table, it is not possible to rank every country against every iceberg factor because information is not available for every country.

Let us look at some of the questions raised for mentoring by the framework. At this stage, it is a good idea to pause and think about the key factors in your organization's culture, as you understand them now. This will provide a 'helicopter' view of your culture to hold in mind as you read through the chapter and to which you can relate the ideas discussed here.

THE ICEBERG FACTORS AND MENTORING

We need to look in more detail at each dimension of culture and its implications for mentoring. (Throughout this section, by 'the line manager', we mean the line manager to whom the mentoree reports in the normal course of their work.)

Change (Low versus High Orientation)

As we suggest in Chapter 1, mentoring's real purpose is to bring about change, individual and organizational. If that is the case, we might expect that cultures which have a high orientation to change

| | 'ICEBERG FACTORS' THAT MAY AFFECT DIFFERENT DIMENSIONS OF MENTORING ||||||||| |
| | ORGANIZATION <- -> INDIVIDUALS ||||||||| |
	CHANGE (low vs high uncertainty avoidance)	POWER (high vs low centralization)	COMMUNICATION FLOW (acceptability outside the hierarchy)	GROUP (vs individual)	STATUS (who you are vs what you do)	EGO (high vs low orientation)	LEADERSHIP (manager as expert vs facilitator)	COMMUNICATION CONTEXT (high vs low)	INVOLVEMENT (high vs low)
LEGITIMACY (of monitoring)									
THE MENTOR									
THE MENTOREE									
THE LINE MANAGER									
THE MENTORING AGREEMENT									
THE MENTORING RELATIONSHIP									
FEEDBACK STYLE									
CONFIDENTIALITY									

Figure 10.1 'Iceberg Factors' that May Affect Different Dimensions of Mentoring

will more readily accept this as an objective of mentoring. Countries which are less oriented to change will be less likely to do so. As a proxy for attitudes to change, we call on the research of Geert Hofstede (1991), who found that societies differ in their propensity for 'uncertainty avoidance'—the extent to which the members of a culture feel threatened by uncertain or unstructured situations and the extent to which they try to avoid these situations. Countries which rank highly on uncertainty avoidance will probably have a low change orientation and vice versa. Societies and organizations with high uncertainty avoidance seek to avoid ambiguity and provide greater structure by establishing formal rules, rejecting deviant ideas and behaviour, and accepting the possibility of absolute truths. Mentoring as a process and as an agent of change may be less readily accepted.

Research on the impact of culture on training may provide some other clues about the impact of uncertainty avoidance on mentoring (Journal of Management Development, 1995). It is suggested that in cultures with weak uncertainty avoidance, trainers are allowed to say 'I don't know' and trainees are comfortable with unanswered questions. They are encouraged to seek innovative approaches to problem solving and intellectual disagreements are viewed as stimulating. Mentoring could find fertile ground in this setting. On the other hand, cultures with strong uncertainty avoidance expect the instructor to have all the answers. Trainers are considered experts, so intellectual disagreements are considered disrespectful. Trainees are rewarded for conformity with trainer-established principles. Mentors in this climate may be expected to provide answers rather than encouraging mentorees to work through problems.

High orientation

Legitimacy of mentoring This type of culture is more likely to ask: 'How do we now progress the mentoring concept? Is it for the individual and/or the organization? What is its focus?' The high orientation to change culture will encourage openness to new ways of working and a more ready acceptance that mentoring can be used in a strategic way as part of the change process.

Mentors They are likely to understand their role as change agents. How can we build on this to help them?

Mentorees   Do they understand the purpose and scope of mentoring as a change process?

Managers of mentoree   With sufficient briefing, they will understand that mentoring does not threaten line authority.

Mentoring agreement   It will be legitimate for all parties to mentoring to contract what is needed from the mentoring relationships.

Low orientation

Legitimacy   Mentoring may not be readily accepted as a strategic intervention which supports the change process.

Mentors   Mentors may have a concern about the focus of mentoring. Is it directed towards the individual, which may be more acceptable, or is it towards the organization?

Mentorees   Will mentorees be adaptable enough to allow mentoring to overcome culture? Will they tend to seek 'answers' rather than think through issues for themselves? Might they see mentoring as a way of breaking the 'old mould'?

Mentorees' manager   More reassurance will be needed that the strangeness or ambiguity involved in introducing mentoring will be tolerated and that it is endorsed by top management.

Mentoring agreement   This will have to be very specific regarding what is involved in mentoring in order to build reassurance that mentoring will not cut out or override the existing structures of the organization. Organizations in this culture may face the issue of confidentiality being viewed more as 'conditional' rather than as 'absolute'. Mentors may, for example, break the confidentiality of the mentoring relationship, deliberately or inadvertently, for an organizational reason or purpose. This would have serious implications for the success of a mentoring initiative unless firmly addressed.

Power (High versus Low Centralization)

Here, we use Hofstede's concept of 'power distance'. Power distance measures the extent to which the less powerful members of a society accept an unequal distribution of power or in which the members of organizations think it is legitimate for most power to be held at the top or centre of the organization. A centralized, autocratic organization has a high level of power distance. A decentralized, participative organization has low power distance.

We suggest that in high power distance societies and organizations, senior managers may not always be willing to share information with more junior people. Information such as that concerning current and future strategy and changes can be important inputs to a mentoring relationship, as they help the mentoree to think about the implications for their career development. In countries with a high power orientation (e.g. France, Spain), mentoring may indeed develop strong connotations of patronage or sponsorship to the detriment of development and learning needs. One of the authors was involved in a consulting assignment with a French Swiss multinational company and was describing the benefits of the mentoring approach to the company's senior HR managers. While the latter were sympathetic to the notion, they worried that in their own organization mentoring could be a means whereby certain powerful senior managers advanced the career interests of their own protégés.

The previously cited research on training in different cultures is again relevant here for its implications about learning through mentoring. It has been suggested that cultures with low power distance value learner-centred learning and place a premium on initiative by the individual. Mentorees in such cultures may have more freedom to be proactive in contacting mentors and working with them in a collaborative learning style.

Cultures with high power distance, on the other hand, value 'trainer-centred' learning. They place a premium on order and learning occurs through gaining knowledge from the expertise of others. Mentorees in high power distance cultures may expect their mentors to act as expert advisers rather than learning facilitators. Mentors, furthermore, may not recognize the potential learning for themselves in mentoring relationships.

High centralization

Legitimacy of mentoring   There is likely to be a resistance to sharing information and expertise. If you are implementing mentoring, the question must be—what are your organizational barriers and how do we tackle them?

Mentors Mentors are likely to be reluctant or simply unaware of the need to share information. This may be the case with long-term strategy.

Mentorees Mentorees may be defensive and think it inappropriate to receive information from senior people in this way. They may feel disloyal to their boss.

Mentorees' manager They will probably be blocking and untrusting and dislike the mentoring process.

Mentoring agreement The implications for the mentoring agreement may be that mentors, if they do get involved, will possibly focus much more on advice rather than being open in sharing information or opinions on organizational developments.

Low centralization

Legitimacy of mentoring In this culture, there are fewer barriers to sharing information.

Mentors Mentors will be much more open and accessible to mentorees.

Mentorees They will expect access to information and opinion and will want to share their own information with mentors.

Mentorees' managers They will need reassurance but are likely to be more open, particularly if mentoring is positioned and seen as inclusive.

Mentoring agreement The focus for the agreement will be around confidentiality between the mentoring partners, and around both advice and sharing information and opinion.

Communication Flow (Acceptability outside the Hierarchy)

The way that communication flows between people and between levels of the organization is an important cultural variable that can affect mentoring. An important aspect of mentoring is that it involves communication outside the individual's direct reporting relationship with their boss.

Research by André Laurent (1983) provides helpful insights into the acceptability of such communication outside the hierarchy in different cultures. Laurent surveyed managers from different countries who were participating in management courses at the international business school INSEAD in France. One of the descriptors of organizational behaviour that he asked respondents to consider stated: 'In order to have efficient work relationships, it is often necessary to bypass the hierarchical line.' Large proportions of managers from Italy (75%), China (66%), Germany (46%), France (42%), Belgium (42%) and Switzerland (41%) disagreed with this statement. Relatively lower proportions of managers from Sweden (22%), the UK (31%), the Netherlands (37%) and the US (32%) disagreed with it.

Laurent (1981) also found that French managers in a survey reacted very strongly against a suggestion that one individual could report to two different bosses while, for example, Swedish and US managers showed fewer objections. For Laurent this meant that the matrix organization was less likely to work in Latin cultures such as France unless they could be translated in hierarchical terms—one real boss plus one or more staff experts. Difficulties with multiple reporting relationships may also be an indicator of potential problems with mentoring relationships.

Anecdotal evidence also points to a possible reaction to mentoring in countries where communication outside the hierarchy is less acceptable. As Laurent's work shows, Italy ranks as one such country. One of the authors was recently advocating the use of learning partners and mentors to an international group of graduate business students. While many of the students reacted favourably to the suggestion that such learning relationships could help them with their career development, it was hotly contested by an Italian student who up until then had remained fairly quiet. When asked why he was against the idea, he said: 'It is not acceptable in my country. It is disloyal to your boss.' So, it is not only the individual's boss who might react unfavourably to direct reports communicating with other senior managers but also the mentorees themselves who might not see it as a legitimate activity.

Low acceptability outside the hierarchy

Legitimacy of mentoring   Mentoring is seen as threatening. This would have to be faced and a strategy for overcoming its worst effects designed prior to introducing the concept of mentoring. The very word mentoring may be anathema.

Mentors   Mentors may be uncomfortable acting outside the hierarchy. They may view the senior versus junior distinction as a real barrier. This will have implications for the matching process in any mentoring scheme. Mentors and mentorees may have to be close in seniority for the mentoring relationship to work.

Mentorees   Mentorees may experience a lack of comfort and have worries about disloyalty to the line manager.

Mentorees' managers   They may feel exposed and threatened by the mentoring relationship and view the process as disloyalty from the mentoree and unwarranted interference from the mentor.

Mentoring agreement   Confidentiality in the mentoring relationship could suffer and become conditional. There is a possibility that both the mentor and mentoree's manager could collude to increase their comfort and to protect the hierarchy. This could effectively destroy the benefit of introducing mentoring if it became widespread in the organization.

High acceptability outside the hierarchy

There is an acceptance that the kind of contact necessary for successful mentoring is valid.

Mentors   They will be open to the concept of mentoring and are less likely to see communication flow as an issue. They will tend to be positively inclusive of people not in their senior group.

Mentorees   They are more likely to expect access to information as well as active support from senior people.

Mentorees' managers   Under normal circumstances and without anything to the contrary coming from the mentor or mentoree, they will be comfortable with the mentoring concept. Care does need to be taken to make sure that they are fully briefed on the aim and structure of the mentoring relationships.

Mentoring agreement   With this kind of culture the confidentiality of the mentoring relationship is likely to be absolute. One would not expect collusion between the mentor and the mentoree's line manager.

Group (versus Individual)

Both Geert Hofstede and Fons Trompenaars have pointed to the importance of differences between societies that value the group above the individual and those that value the individual above the group. As Hofstede (1991) says:

> The vast majority of people in our world live in societies in which the interest of the group prevails over the interest of the individual. . . . A minority of people in our world live in societies in which the interests of the individual will prevail over the interests of the group. . . . Management techniques and training packages have almost exclusively been developed in individualist countries, and they are based on cultural assumptions which may not hold in collectivist cultures.

Trompenaars (1993) adds:

> Western theories of motivation have individuals growing out of early, and hence primitive, social needs into an individually resplendent self-actualization at the summit of the hierarchy. Needless to say, this does not achieve resonance the world over, however good a theory it may be for America and north-west Europe. The Japanese notion of the highest good is harmonious relationships within and with the patterns of nature; the primary orientation is to other people and to the natural world.

Hofstede points to some basic differences between collectivist and individualist cultures. In collectivist cultures, identity is based in the social network to which one belongs, people think in terms of 'we', harmony should be maintained and direct confrontations avoided, the purpose of education is learning how to do, the relationship between employer and employee is perceived in moral terms like a family link, and relationship prevails over task. In individualist cultures, identity is based in the individual, people think in terms of 'I', speaking one's mind is a characteristic of an honest person, the purpose of education is learning how to learn, the employer–employee relationship is a contract based on mutual advantage, and task prevails over relationship.

Trompenaars also suggests that individualists use methods of individual incentives, such as pay for performance, individual assessment and management by objectives, whereas collectivists give attention to *esprit de corps*, morale and cohesiveness. (In a later book (1993), Hampden-Turner and Trompenaars prefer to use the term 'communitarian', rather than collectivist, to describe group-oriented societies.)

The group versus individual dimension may be one of the most difficult for mentoring to address. Is it that mentoring as an activity that places high value on individual development, albeit with a strategic purpose, may be more readily accepted in countries with high scores on individualism? Does it cut across collectivist values by making certain individuals stand out from the group? Certainly, mentoring has so far seen its widest application in the US and UK, both countries which rank low on group orientation and high on individualism.

High individual orientation versus group

Legitimacy of mentoring   Mentoring will be seen as a legitimate way for the individual to 'get on'. The mentoring relationship may be influenced by a strong element of sponsorship.

Mentors   Mentors may see mentoring principally as developing high-potential individuals. This may lead to charges of élitism within the organization, which may need to be countered by those responsible for the mentoring initiative.

Mentorees   They may see mentoring solely in terms of personal development. They may need help to see the wider organizational case and to buy in to this.

Mentorees' managers   They may see mentoring as reinforcing their sponsoring role. They will think in terms of participating in a high-potential, individual-focused, possibly élitist initiative. This could cause them problems with those not included for mentoring and so the organization may experience some resistance to this, even in a highly individualistic culture.

Mentoring agreement   The implications for the mentoring agreement are minimal, in that the parties to the mentoring relationship will see it as totally confidential and the concern of those involved. They will see mentoring as having little impact on others in the organization.

High group orientation versus individual

Legitimacy   Mentoring may encounter problems in obtaining legitimacy; it may be seen as encouraging favouritism and being potentially divisive.

Mentors   They will be comfortable with a model of mentoring that highlights an inclusive, possibly team, approach. They may be reluctant to support the individual at the expense of the group.

Mentorees   They may find the mentoring relationship uncomfortable. They may shy away from initiating meetings with mentors, which could effectively 'kill off' mentoring where mentors leave it up to the mentorees to approach them.

Mentorees' managers   Like the mentors, the managers may be reluctant to support individuals at the expense of their group or teams. As support by line management is crucial to the success of organizational mentoring, this group may need to be influenced to see the positive benefits of mentoring, but will need reassurance that it will not have negative effects on their team building and management of their people. This is where managers will often say that mentoring 'does not fit our culture'.

Mentoring agreement   The agreement will need to highlight the potential for conflict/envy.

Status (Who You Are versus What You Do)

Different attitudes to status are another cultural variable with implications for mentoring. As Fons Trompenaars (1993) says: 'All societies give certain of their members higher status than others, signalling that unusual attention should be focused upon such persons and their activities.' According to Trompenaars, some societies accord status to people on the basis of their achievements— *achieved* status—while other societies ascribe it to them by virtue of age, class, gender, social connections, education, profession etc.— *ascribed* status. Trompenaars' research finds a correlation between Protestantism and achievement orientation, with Catholic, Buddhist and Hindu cultures scoring highly on ascription.

One way in which achievement versus ascription might affect mentoring concerns the expectations that mentorees might have about the kind of mentors with whom they should work. For example, as noted, a particularly important aspect of the status dimension that has relevance for mentoring is age, particularly where companies are considering its use in an Asian context. An article in *Management Today* (Lewis, 1996) reports that there is a saying in Korea that 'if you're not 40, you're nobody'. In Korean companies, according to the article, it is expected that important decisions should be left to the mature and experienced. 'Exaggerated' respect for age in China, Japan and Korea is said to stem from the principles of Confucianism. These include an emphasis on education, titles, thrift, moderation, kindliness and respect for seniority. 'People under 40, whatever their reputation or brilliance, strike Asians as being junior and inexperienced.' Individuals may expect to be mentored by much older mentors.

Low status (what you are)

Legitimacy Mentoring will be seen as a legitimate way of pushing forward the development of the individual and as validly focused on personal achievement.

Mentors They are likely be chosen because they are high achievers.

Mentorees They will look to high-achieving mentors to become career enhancers.

Mentorees' managers They may have a sense of competing with the mentoree. There may be unease at the link between the high-performing mentor and the mentoree. They may see mentorees as threatening their position.

Mentoring agreement The whole process of the mentoring relationship can be less formal and much more *ad hoc* in terms of meetings and timings.

High status (who you are)

Legitimacy The role of mentor may be seen as part of the territory of being a senior manager. The type of mentoring may become much more a sponsorship model with an emphasis on assisting the mentor in building a power base in the organization. A mentor in this culture may have several mentorees.

Mentors They may expect to conform to a management role model of how to get on in the organization. They may see themselves as sponsors and replicating a replacement management structure in their image for management succession purposes.

Mentorees They may expect to conform to a management role model to 'get on' in the organization. This model may seem to be about 'cloning' replacement managers for management succession purposes.

Mentorees' managers They may be more comfortable than their opposite numbers in the low-status culture because of a more secure 'ascribed' status as managers in the organization *vis à vis* the mentoree.

Mentoring agreement The mentoring processes may be more company based or 'political'. They may be more formal and encourage 'power games' or 'politicking'. Confidentiality will be a significant factor in the success of mentoring relationships.

Ego (High versus Low Orientation)

One of the dimensions of cultural difference identified by Geert Hofstede (1991) concerns what he calls 'masculine versus feminine'. He defines masculinity as the extent to which the dominant values in a culture emphasize assertiveness and materialism, while not particularly reflecting concern for people. Femininity is the extent to which the dominant values emphasize relationships between people, concern for others, and the overall quality of life. We are not totally comfortable with the masculine/feminine label but have yet to find a satisfactory replacement. For the moment, we prefer to talk about high versus low ego cultures.

Outside the US and the UK, one region where mentoring has been taken up enthusiastically is Scandinavia, as some of our case studies indicate. According to Hofstede, the Scandinavian cultures rank as societies with the strongest 'feminine-oriented' values, or what we prefer to call low ego cultures. Management researchers Peter Lawrence and Tony Spybey (1986) likewise describe 'the satisfaction Swedes get from being part of progressiveness' and 'from taking a stand against the ills of the world.'

Concern for the quality of work life (of which the innovative work groups at Volvo are one of the best-known examples) provides fertile ground for mentoring in Scandinavia. Over and above its benefits in developing high-potential individuals and in contributing to strategy and organizational development, mentoring may be seen in Scandinavia as a valuable approach in itself. ABB Sweden's mentoring scheme, which caters for both blue- and white-collar workers, reflects such a view. ABB Sweden's vision is, indeed, that everyone in the company should have a mentor. Scandinavian organizations have introduced some very successful mentoring schemes for women, such as the programme at Ericsson and the Ruter Dam (Queen of Diamonds) scheme which links women managers with mentors in other companies.

Low ego culture

Legitimacy There may be more tolerance for perceptions of 'dependence' than in a high ego culture, even though mentoring is not about building dependence.

Mentors They will naturally seek out their roles. There will be a readiness to support and to exchange learning.

Mentorees They may expect support from the mentoring relationship, but may not receive a high degree of challenge.

Mentorees' managers   They are more likely to be cooperative and less competitive with the mentoree.

Mentoring agreement   The processes of the mentoring relationship will be more two way. There will be better chances of absolute confidentiality and the mentor's style may be more facilitative—asking, not telling.

High ego culture

Legitimacy of mentoring   It is difficult to accept mentoring if it is perceived as 'dependency'. It may be seen as something that is more directive and a duty of top managers in building a following in the upper echelons of the organization.

Mentors   They may see their role as being more to challenge mentorees rather than to support them.

Mentorees   The mentorees will not expect support and they may find it difficult to confide in senior managers as mentors in this culture. They will see themselves being assessed, albeit informally.

Mentorees' managers   They may feel threatened by the mentoring relationship and may be competitive with the mentorees.

Mentoring agreement   There may be a temptation for the mentors to assess the mentorees informally, which could make any confidentiality conditional rather than absolute. Much of the content of the mentoring conversations could be more around telling rather than asking and may be very anecdotal. The process may be seen by mentors as less two way.

Leadership (Manager as Expert versus Facilitator)

Differing attitudes to leadership in different cultures may also have implications for mentoring. In particular, they raise questions concerning expectations about the learning relationship between mentor and mentoree.

One of the statements that André Laurent (1983) of INSEAD put to his respondents was designed to identify whether people expect their managers to be experts or to play more of a facilitative, coaching role. The statement was as follows: 'It is important for a manager to have at hand precise answers to most of the questions that his subordinates may raise about their work'. Responses to the statement showed wide variations in the way that people from different countries view the role of the manager. Countries where only relatively few people agreed with the statement (i.e. those where managers may be expected to play a more facilitative role) were Sweden (10%), the Netherlands (17%), the US (18%), Denmark (23%) and the UK (27%). Countries where a relatively high proportion of people agreed with the statement (i.e. those expecting the manager to be an expert) included Germany (46%), France (53%), Italy (66%), China (74%) and Japan (78%).

The implication of these findings for mentoring is that in countries with a manager-as-expert orientation, the mentor too may expect to play an expert role in the mentoring relationship. The mentoree may also expect the mentor to provide them with solutions to problems, rather than helping them to think through and make sense of the issues themselves.

Low expert orientation (manager as facilitator)

Legitimacy of mentoring The role of management as facilitators of learning should be recognized. This will give great legitimacy to the establishment of mentoring.

Mentors They will regard mentoring as a natural extension of their roles.

Mentorees They will seek mutual learning opportunities and share information and understanding.

Mentorees' managers They will view mentoring as an inclusive and positive relationship which helps individual and organizational learning.

Mentoring agreement The balance of the relationship will be more equal and will be about mutual learning and sharing. There will be an empowered feel to these mentoring relationships.

High expert orientation (manager as expert)

Legitimacy of mentoring   Mentoring may be much more a coaching model. Mentors may feel that they are not equipped to be mentors unless they have expert knowledge. They may feel that the mentoring relationship should have a 'hard', task-centred focus. Too strong a coaching focus could lead to problems with the line, as mentoring may then infringe on task and resource issues.

Mentors   They will act like coaches and be comfortable in this mode.

Mentorees   They may become more passive in this type of culture and see the mentoree's role as receiving wisdom from the mentor.

Mentorees' managers   They may be distrustful and uneasy if the coaching model of mentoring is implemented. There is a potential for conflict if this cultural issue is not addressed. The manager may see mentoring as irrelevant because they are the manager and therefore the expert.

Mentoring agreement   The style of the mentoring relationships will be more didactic and less empowered from the mentorees' perspective.

Communication Context (High versus Low)

Effective communication between mentor and mentoree is clearly a vital factor in successful mentoring. Culture may also have a powerful influence here. Research by Edward T. Hall and Mildred Reed Hall (1990) points to the importance of the context in which communication takes place in different cultures. They distinguish in particular between high context and low context communication. A high context communication is one in which little has to be said or written because most of the information is either in the physical environment or within the person, while very little is in the coded, explicit part of the message.

Low context communications hold most of the information in the message itself, while high context communications are much more subjective. The meaning is deeply influenced by mutual understanding about relationships, history and status. In high context cultures, verbal messages have little meaning without the surrounding context. In low context cultures, the message is everything.

Collectivist cultures tend to have high context communication, while individualist cultures have low context communication, according to Hofstede (1991). American consultants Copeland and Griggs (1985) identify Japan, China and Arab countries as high context cultures, while the Scandinavian countries and Germany are the strongest low context cultures. A perfect example of high context communication was described in the *New York Times* (Haberman, 1988):

> Many Japanese managers are convinced they can communicate with each other without words at all. It is called 'Haragei' or 'Belly language' because of the country's cultural homogeneity . . . Japanese can somehow convey their intentions through penetrating stares, casual glances, occasional grunts and meaningful silences. As a rule foreigners are beyond such communication.'

The further apart on the context scale that people are, the more difficult it is to communicate between them. High context cultures do not want or expect, and are irritated by, detailed information. Information is shared with everyone, relationships are more important than objective data, there is an overlap between business and social relationships, and authority and status are more important than competence. High context cultures are comfortable in a sea of information. On the other hand, low context cultures place heavy reliance on detailed background and information, centralize information, are more objective and information based than relationship based, compartmentalize business and social relationships, and emphasize competence above position and status. They may suffer overload if information flows in a rapid, disorganized way.

The impact of these differences on mentoring could be considerable, particularly in cross-border mentoring. Matching mentors and mentorees from high and low context cultures may well produce unforeseen communication difficulties, especially when they are far apart on the context scale. At its most extreme, what happens when a quiet Japanese mentoree is matched with a direct German mentor?

Low communication context

Legitimacy of mentoring   There may be more need for mentoring in a low context culture where more explanation about the background for decision making could be necessary. Paradoxically, a low context culture may make it more difficult to implement a mentoring approach in the organization.

Mentors   They may give feedback that will be more direct and detailed. Although communication is more explicit, the mentor can still add value by providing context about the way in which decisions are made (one of the primary functions of an organizational mentor). They may need to be slightly 'counter cultural' to do this.

Mentorees   They will have to be robust individuals, able to work with the feedback style of the organization.

Mentorees' managers   They will reinforce the low context style and culture and will need development in appreciating the issues around this style if mentoring is to be introduced into the organization successfully.

Mentoring agreement   There will be more requirement for specific needs to be stated explicitly in discussions.

High communication context

Legitimacy of mentoring   There may be more resistance to mentoring where communication is high context. The mentoring relationships may share more personal information in this type of culture.

Mentors   Mentors with high position and access to quality information will be sought by mentorees. Feedback styles will be very indirect.

Mentorees   They need to be very attuned and sensitive to the messages behind what is stated. Good organizational antennae are required.

Mentorees' managers   They will reinforce the culture that exists in the organization. They may be more comfortable with a mentoring role which reinforces organizational messages to the mentoree. There is some potential for collusion between mentors and managers here.

Mentoring agreement   Less will be stated explicitly in the mentoring agreement between the parties.

Involvement (High versus Low Orientation)

We noted that high context cultures tend to have overlapping business and social relationships while low context cultures tend to compartmentalize them. This leads us to the final dimension of cultural difference discussed here—the degree to which people in organizations in different societies get involved with each other.

We turn again to the work of Fons Trompenaars (1993) who points to the difference between 'specific' and 'diffuse' cultures. In specific-oriented cultures, 'the manager segregates out the task relationship that he or she has with a subordinate and insulates this from other dealings'. Were the manager to meet a subordinate outside work, none of the authority would 'diffuse' itself into the relationship. However, diffuse-oriented cultures, says Trompenaars, are those where 'every life space and every level of personality tends to permeate all the others. . . . [in France] *Monsieur le directeur* is a formidable authority wherever you encounter him.' Trompenaars cites the work of psychologist Kurt Lewin who suggests that people have private and public 'life spaces'. Cultures differ in the relative size of these spaces and the degree to which people let others into their private space. Americans, for example, have much more public than private space, while Germans have a relatively small public space and a large private space which it is difficult for others to enter.

The specific–diffuse distinction gives us some clues as to how mentoring relationships might work in different societies. In specific-oriented cultures, we might expect mentoring relationships to focus on work and career issues. In diffuse-oriented cultures, relationships might well become closer and spread beyond work issues. The distinction may be particularly important in feedback. In relationships with diffuse cultures, direct speech can be insulting where loss of face is involved.

Low involvement

Legitimacy of mentoring   Mentoring will have legitimacy if it is seen as mainly work focused.

Mentors   They will regard the mentoring relationship as work oriented and will value a more distant relationship with the mentoree. This detachment may actually promote better perspective and objectivity for the mentor and need not be viewed negatively.

Mentorees   Discussion of personal issues could be viewed as a 'weakness'. There may be less openness in mentoring relationships in this culture.

Mentorees' managers   They will probably not want involvement in the mentoring relationship, but may be suspicious of the greater involvement of senior management promoted by a mentoring initiative.

Mentoring agreement   The agreement may be more specific and work centred.

High involvement

Legitimacy of mentoring   The concept will be accepted more easily. Personal as well as work issues will be on the agenda on the basis of 'the whole person comes to work' approach.

Mentors   They will be open to discussion of wider issues. A potential danger is that the mentor could get so involved with the mentoree that they lose the organizational purpose and objectivity in the mentoring relationship.

Mentorees   They may be concerned not to 'lose face' and prefer indirect feedback.

Mentorees' managers   They may seek more active involvement in the relationship.

Mentoring agreement   The agenda will be wide and could involve the line manager more directly. The process of the mentoring relationship could take longer, with more meetings taking place than in low involvement cultures.

APPLYING THE ICEBERG FRAMEWORK

So how can the framework of cultural iceberg factors be used in practice? Participants in our international mentoring workshops have derived a number of general lessons from the model. One participant said that it indicates the need to be wary of mixing extremes of distance and culture in an international mentoring relationship. Another participant suggested that perhaps the way to start is to create mentoring relationships between cultures with similar clusters of attributes—a more evolutionary way of fostering transnationalism.

Implementing mentoring internationally often means managing the tension between the macro-level understanding of the benefits of a mentoring approach held by senior managers and HR specialists with international experience and the micro level representing strong constraints deeper down in the organization.

What does the iceberg framework tell us about potential issues that need to be taken into account in this situation? It indicates in particular that the organization is likely to be less open to new concepts and that power and information are likely to be quite highly centralized. It tells us that status considerations are probably important and that managers are more likely to expect to play an expert rather than a facilitative role. Relationships between people are also more likely to be task oriented.

The model highlights the need to pay special attention to certain aspects of implementing a mentoring approach. First, the HR managers have to present a particularly strong business case to sell the mentoring scheme to management influencers, including middle and regional managers. Another key lesson that has emerged is the requirement for effective and constant involvement of senior management stakeholders in the process. One of the most practical learning points here is that the organization must take great care with prior communication about the scheme and the stakeholders' role in it. When explanations are not sufficiently provided, people project their own explanations into the gap.

Written communications may not always convey the intended message, particularly when they concern a new way of doing things that people may initially view as counter cultural. It is important to spend more time on one-to-one communication with stakeholders before the process goes too far. This helps to obtain effective buy-in to the project.

The organization should aim to start with a pilot scheme that can be used as a platform to cascade the mentoring approach later on if appropriate.

MENTORING AS A CULTURAL CHANGE AGENT

As we have said, the cultural framework is a launchpad for questions. The answers are not black and white. It is for you, as organizational specialists, to identify the parameters that need to be addressed in deciding on success criteria for mentoring in your own organizational context. It is clear that attention to the process is vital. This is important in whatever context you introduce mentoring, whether in a domestic setting or abroad. However, as in all international activities where culture is likely to have an impact, we need to consider the process in even more depth and manage it even more carefully.

It is also clear that we must not expect things to work the same way everywhere. Individual organizations must establish for themselves the degree to which local HR management in their operations are allowed to adapt the mentoring scheme to fit their business culture.

In an international organization, it is true that the impact of many of the cultural iceberg factors may be moderated by corporate values that are shared across borders. We also know that at senior levels of management, multi-country managers with much international experience tend to have developed some common values, irrespective of their country of origin, particularly with regard to attitudes toward learning. However, deep down in the operations of an international company, or where senior managers have not had significant international exposure, the impact of the iceberg factors on any mentoring initiative is still likely to be important. The culture framework presented here aims to help those involved in mentoring schemes to work through some of the potential issues.

As we have emphasized, the model here is indicative only. It is a starting point for thinking about differences and their implications, but is not a substitute for learning in more depth about culture and its impact on HR policies.

Ultimately, however, we believe that mentoring is about making managers and organizations more competitive in the global business arena. This does involve change and mentoring is a change process. Culture is not static, nor is it an absolute given. As we noted in the last chapter, one of the competencies of the successful international manager is the ability to bring about change and to stretch the boundaries in different cultural contexts. Mentoring across borders will always involve managing the balance between accepting cultural constraints on the process and working to mitigate them.

SELF-ASSESSMENT

- Are your organization and its managers fully aware of the impact of culture on its operations?
- Is mentoring an option for you in your international environment?
- Will your mentoring approach be up to the challenges of culture?
- How will you deal with the iceberg factors?
- Will your mentoring approach support change and reinforce the organizational strategy?
- Can you identify cultures/countries where mentoring may flourish more easily to start with and which could offer some early wins for the mentoring concept?

Chapter 11

Implementing Mentoring Internationally

We summarize here our learning to date with regard to this new international development approach. We also set out a checklist based on our knowledge of taking mentoring into the international dimension.

KEY LEARNING AND QUESTIONS ABOUT INTERNATIONAL MENTORING

International mentoring may manifest itself in a way that reflects a learning or a control cultural orientation. Where are you on Figure 11.1?

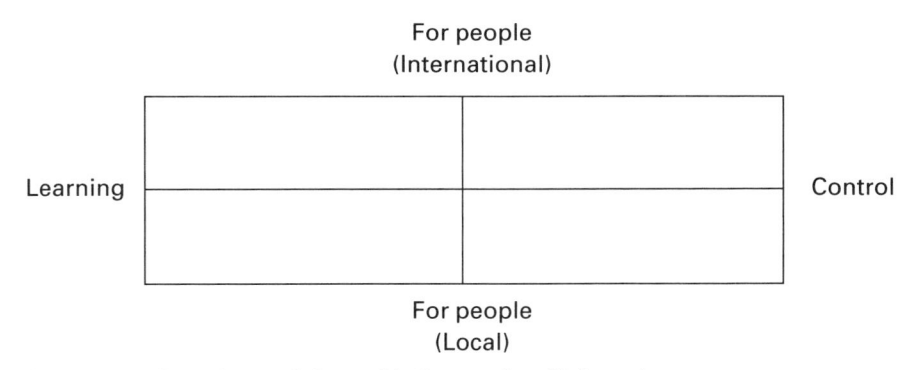

Figure 11.1 Learning and Control in International Mentoring

- We know that mentoring, properly implemented, can help the development of both the organization and individuals.
- Mentoring is a strategic intervention, not a 'bolt-on' approach.
- For international managers, there is often a gap in terms of a lack of opportunities for reflection. Mentoring is an opportunity for significant reflection via dialogue with a learning partner. Find ways to build mentoring into the international management development process. Mentoring has a potential role in turning international assignments into real learning experiences for the individual, the mentor and the organization.
- Mentoring can help in building a global mindset and global perspectives by assigning mentors from another country/culture or even function.
- Mentors can provide greater organizational integration/synergy by linking mentors/mentorees across international/cultural organizational boundaries.
- Mentoring needs to take account of the potential impact of cultural differences. There is no rigid prescription for mentoring internationally.
- The impact of cultural differences may be lessened in the higher echelons of international management.
- At a lower organizational level in multinational companies, the impact of cultural differences may have a stronger impact on different dimensions of mentoring.
- At higher levels, be aware of how you match people across borders.
- International mentoring can have a cross-border international management development focus or a local management development focus. Therefore, are you developing international managers *or* using mentoring to develop the local organization?
- There may be a continuum of ease of implementation of mentoring across different cultural boundaries, depending on the purpose of mentoring.
- A clear, well-constructed strategy that includes developing mentors/mentorees and line management is necessary for the successful implementation of mentoring.
- A strategy for coping with time and geography is essential for distance mentoring.

A CHECKLIST FOR IMPLEMENTING INTERNATIONAL MENTORING

Before: Creating an International Mentoring Programme

- Assess the business case for international mentoring:
  - Why do individuals and the organization need an international mentoring programme?
  - What are your organizational strategic objectives and how can mentoring support them?
  - Are you developing international perspectives?
  - Are you developing a cadre of international managers?
  - Are you using mentoring to support international assignments?
  - Are you assisting re-entry?
  - Are you supporting learning?
  - Are you creating synergy and integration in international operations?
  - Can mentoring be integrated with existing international development programmes?
- Make the business case to major stakeholders to win support.
- Establish a set of objectives for your international mentoring programme. Success criteria might be:
  - Decrease in number of expatriate failures
  - Better international assignment process
  - Faster integration and higher performance from assignees
  - Better re-entry to home organization
  - More assignments abroad
  - More willingness to accept overseas assignments among management
  - Better retention of top performers
- Set out who is involved in the mentoring programme and why. Set priorities.
- Secure top management buy-in. Influence champions—but do not oversell the initiative.
- Clarify the operational aspects of the programme—costs, programme coordinators etc.
- Identify mentor and mentoree population based on need.
- Design the scheme. Set out the parameters and organizational mentoring contract.
- Start small and grow the programme organically.

- Address the distance and time issues and potential solutions.
- Think through the iceberg factors in your scenario.
- Benchlearn with others who are using this approach—learn directly from their experiences.

During: Operating an International Mentoring Programme

- Provide information about the objectives of the programme, how it will operate and what is expected. Work through the issues in the Mentoring Contract.
- Run workshops for mentors, mentorees and line people. Include the cultural issues appropriately. Address the time and distance issues directly.
- Set the core approach from which local operations can propose their individual approaches. Check that these are consistent with the objectives of your mentoring programme overall.
- Foster line support for the international mentoring programme and reassure line concerns.
- Be aware of mismatches in the mentoring relationships.
- Use mentorees as mentors where appropriate in growing the mentoring approach.

After: Monitoring and Evaluating an International Mentoring Programme

- Where possible, use an external expert to carry out individual qualitative interviews to give a true picture of people's experience and at the same time preserve the confidentiality and privacy of the mentoring relationships.
- Monitor discreetly—do not supervise or intrude.
- Evaluate the strategic effect on the business objectives, not the success of the programme itself.
- Brief top management on progress and results.
- Broadcast sensibly and use news of success to expand the mentoring initiative appropriately.

Now over to you. We wish you success if you decide on the mentoring approach in your organization.

Bibliography and Further Reading

Adler, N. (1991) *International Dimensions of Organizational Behavior*, PWS-Kent Publishing, Boston, MA.
Alexander, Raymond S. and Brisbon, Delores (1993) 'Diversity in Hospital Management—A Diagnosis and Prescription', *Trustee* (TST), Vol. 46, 7 (July).
Alleman, E. (1983) *Measuring Mentoring: A Manual for the Leadership Development Questionnaire*, LD Consultants, Ohio.
Alleman, E., et al (1984) 'Enriching Mentoring Relationships', *The Personnel and Guidance Journal*, Vol. 32, 9 (February).
Arndt, S. (1989) 'Mentor Programs Help Boost Production', *National Underwriter*, Vol. 93, 5.
Arnold, V. and Davidson, M.J. (1990) 'Adopt a Mentor: The New Way Ahead for Women Managers', *Women in Management Review and Abstracts*, Vol. 5, 1.
Ball, A.L. (1989) 'Mentors and Protégés: Portraits of Success', *Working Woman*, 134, 142 (October).
Barham, K. and Devine, M. (1991) *The Quest for the International Manager*, The Economist Intelligence Unit, London.
Barham, K. and Oates, D. (1991) *The International Manager*, Economist Books, London.
Barham, K., Fraser, J. and Heath, L. (1988) *Management for the Future*, Ashridge Management Research Group, Berkhamsted.
Barks, J.B. and Vocino, J. (1988) 'Career Wastelands: The Way Out', *Distribution*, Vol. 87, 3.
Baum, Howell S. (1992) 'Mentoring: Narcissistic Fantasies and Oedipal Realities', *Human Relations*.
Berthoin Antal, A. (1993) 'Odysseus' Legacy to Management Development', *European Management Journal*, Vol. 11, 4, pp 448–54.
Bolton, E.B. (1980) 'A Conceptual Analysis of the Mentor Relationship in the Career Development of Women', *Adult Education*, Vol. 30, 4, pp 195–207.
Boston (1976) *The Sorcerer's Apprentice: A Case Study in the Role of the Mentor*, Council for Exceptional Children, Reston, BA.
Bowen, D.D. (1982) 'On Considering Aspects of the Mentoring Process', *Behaviour Today*, Vol. 13, 15, pp 4–5.

Bowen, D.D. (1986) 'The Role of Identification in Mentoring Female Protégées', *Group & Organizational Studies*, Vol. 11, 1–2.

Bragg, A. (1989) 'Is a Mentor Program in Your Future?' *Sales and Marketing Management*, Vol. 141, 11 (September).

Bray, D., Campbell R. and Grant, D. (1974) *Formative Years in Business: A Long Term Study of Managerial Lives*, Wiley, New York.

Brennan, Mairin (1993) 'Graduate Level: a Mixed Picture for Minorities', *Chemical and Engineering News* (CEN), Vol. 71, 37 (September).

Brown, R.L. (1990) 'Mentoring Program Builds $1m Agencies', *Managers Magazine*, Vol. 65, 5 (May).

Brown, Robert L. (1993) 'Start with Structure: Creating a Mentoring Program', *Managers Magazine*, Vol. 68 (January).

Brown, T. (1990) 'Match Up with a Mentor', *Industry Week*, Vol. 239, 19 (October).

Buonocore, A.J. (1987) 'Reducing the Turnover of New Hires', *Journal of Management Solutions*, Vol. 32, 6.

Burke, R.J. and McKeen, C.A. (1989) 'Developing Formal Mentoring Programmes in Organizations', *Business Quarterly* (Canada), Vol. 53, 3 (Winter).

Burke, R.J. and McKeen, C.A. (1990) 'Mentoring in Organizations: Implications for Women', *Journal of Business Ethics* (Netherlands), Vol. 9.

Calvacca, L. (1989) 'Mentor Watch: How to Manage the Search', *Working Women*.

Carp, H.B. (1989) 'Supervising the Plateaued Worker', *Supervisory Management*, Vol. 34, 6.

Carsrud, A.L. et al (1987) 'Entrepreneurs, Mentors, Networks and Successful New Venture Development: An Exploratory Study', *American Journal of Small Business*, Vol. 12, 2 (Autumn).

Chao G.T. and O'Leary, A.M. (in press) 'Third-party perceptions toward Mentorship: An explanation of same and cross-gender Mentoring', *Mentoring International*, Vancouver, British Columbia.

Chao, Georgia, et al. (1992) 'Formal and Informal Mentorships', *Personnel Psychology*, Vol. 45.

Clawson, J. (1980) 'Mentoring in Managerial Careers', in C.B Devv (Ed.) *Work, Family and the Career*, Praeger, New York, pp 144–165.

Clawson, J. and Kram, K. (1984) 'Managing X-gender mentoring', *Business Horizons*, Vol. 27, 3, pp 22–32.

Collin, A. (1988) 'Mentoring', *Industrial and Commercial Training* (UK), Vol. 20, 2.

Collins, E.G.C. and Scott, P. (1978) 'Everyone Who Makes it Has a Mentor', *Harvard Business Review*.

Colwill, N.L. (1984) 'Mentors and Protégés, Women and Men', *Business Quarterly*, Vol. 42, 2.

Copeland, L. and Griggs, L. (1985) *Going International: How to Make Friends and Deal Effectively in the Global Marketplace*, Random House, New York.

Crainer, Stuart (1995) 'Local Learning in a Global Market', *Financial Times*, 2 June.

Dalton, G., Thompson, P. and Price, R. (1977) 'The Four Stages of Professional Careers: A New Look at Performance by Professionals', *Organizational Dynamics*, Vol. 6, 1.

Davis, R.L. (1979) 'Mentoring: In Search of a Taxonomy', Garrison, P.A. Master's Thesis, MIT Sloan School of Business.

Dolan, Thomas C. (1993) 'Mentoring in the 1990s', *Health Executive* (HEE), Vol. 8, 6 (November/December).

Drackby, D. (1989) 'Rewards Make the Mentor', *Personnel*, Vol. 66, 12.

Dreher, G.F. and Ash, R.A. (1990) 'A Comparative Study of Mentoring among Men and Women in Managerial, Professional and Technical Positions', *Journal of Applied Psychology*, Vol. 75, 5.

Dunbar, D. (1990) 'Desperately Seeking Mentors', *Black Enterprise*, Vol. 20 (8 March), pp 53–6.

Fagenson, E.A. (1989) 'The Mentor Advantage: Perceived job/career experiences of protégés vs. non-protégés', *Journal of Occupational Behaviour*, Vol. 10, pp 309–20.

Falletti, P.F. (1987) 'How to Stimulate New Directors', *Journal of Directors and Boards*, Vol. 11, 4.

Farren, C. et al. (1984) 'Mentoring: A Boon to Career Development', *Personnel*, Nov/Dec.

Fury, K (1980) 'Mentor Mania', *Savvy*, pp 42–7.

Gabarro, J. (1979) 'Socializations at the Top: How CCOs and Subordinates Evolve Interpersonal Contacts', *Organization Dynamics*, Winter.

Gallese, Liz Roman (1993) 'Do Women Make Poor Mentors?', *Across the Board* (CBR), Vol. 30, 6 (July/August).

George, P. and Kummerow, J. (1981) 'Mentoring for Career Women', *Training/HRD*.

Granfield, Mary (1993) 'Mentoring for Money', *Working Women*, Vol. 1 (March).

Grant, J. (1988) 'Women as Managers: What They Can Offer to Organizations', *Organization Dynamics*, Vol. 16, 3.

Gray and Gray M.M. (eds) (1986) 'Mentoring: Aid to Excellence', Vol. 1, 2, *Proceedings of the First International Conference on Mentoring*, Vancouver (21–25 July).

Green, T.B. and Knippen J.T. (1991) 'Every Boss Has a Style', *Management Decision*, Vol. 29, 5.

Haberman, C. (1988) 'Some Japanese (One) Urge Plain Speaking', *New York Times*, 27 March, p. 3.

Hall, Edward T. and Hall, Mildred Reed (1990) *Understanding Cultural Differences: Germans, French and Americans*, Intercultural Press, Yarmouth, Maine.

Hampden-Turner, C. and Trompenaars, F. (1993) *The Seven Cultures of Capitalism*, Doubleday, New York.
Handy, C. (1985) *Understanding Organizations*, Pelican, Harmondsworth.
Harrigan, B.L. (1977) *Games Mother Never Taught You*, Rawson Associates, New York.
Harrison, R. (1987) *Organization Culture and Quality of Service: A Strategy for Releasing Love in the Workplace*, AMED, London.
Henderson, D.W. (1985) 'Enlightened Mentoring: A Characteristic of Public Management Professionalism', *Public Administration Review*, Vol. 45, 6.
Hennefrund, W. (1986) 'Taking the Measure of Mentoring', *Association Management*, Vol. 38, 1 (January).
Herman, J.S. (1980) 'Mentoring: A tool for empowering women', Summary proceedings, *Mentoring*, a conference for women leaders of New York's State and Academic communities, Institute for Education and Research on Women and Work, 10–18.
Hill, S. et al (1989) 'Mentoring and other Communication Support in the Academic Setting', *Group and Organizational Studies*, Vol. 14.3, September.
Hofstede, G. (1991) *Cultures and Organizations: Software of the Mind*, McGraw-Hill, London.
Hunt, D.M. and Michael, C. (1983) 'Mentoring: A Career Training and Development Tool', *Academy of Management Review*, Vol. 8, 3.
Industrial Society (1992) *Training Survey No. 4*, London.
Ioannou, L. (1995) 'Stateless Executives', *International Business*, Feb., pp 48–52.
Jacoby, D. (1989) 'Rewards Make the Mentor', *Personnel*, Vol. 66, 12 (December), pp 10–14.
Johnson, M.C. (1988) 'Mentors: the Key to Development and Growth', *Training and Development Journal*, July.
Journal of Management Development (1995) 'Training across Cultures', Vol. 14, 9, pp 57–9.
Journal of Management Solutions (1987) 'A Matter of Personal Ability not Gender', Vol. 32, 11.
Kanter, R.M. (1977) *Men and Women of the Corporation*, Basic Books, New York.
Keele, R.L. (1987) Buckner, et al. 'Formal Mentoring Programs Are no Panacea', *Management Review*, Vol. 76, 2 (February).
King, M. (1990) 'Ambition on Trial', *Black Enterprise*, Vol. 20, 7.
Kinsey, D.C. (1990) 'Mentorship and Influence in Nursing', *Nursing Management*, Vol. 21 (5 May), pp 45–6.
Kizilos, P. (1990) 'Take my Mentor, Please!', *Training*, Vol. 2, 7 (4 April), pp 49–55.
Klopf, G.J. and Harrison, J. (1982) 'The Case for Mentors', *Education Digest*.

Knippen and Green (1991) 'Developing a Mentoring Relationship', *Management Decision* 2.
Kolb, D.A. (1984) *Experiential Learning: Experience as the Source of Learning and Development*, Prentice Hall, Englewood Cliffs, NJ.
Kram, K.E. (1980) 'Mentoring Processes at Work: Developmental Relationships in Managerial Careers', doctoral dissertation, Yale University.
Kram, K.E. (1983) 'Phases of the Mentor Relationship', *Academy of Management Journal*, Vol. 26, 4, pp 608–25.
Kram, K.E. (1988) *Mentoring at Work: Developmental Relationships in Organizational Life*, University Press of America, Lanham, MD.
Kram, K.E. and Brager, M.C. (in press) *Development through Mentoring: A Strategic Approach for the 1990s: Theory and Practice*, Charles C. Thomas, Springfield, IL.
Kram, K.E. and Hall, D.T. (1989) 'Mentoring as an Antidote to Stress during Corporate Trauma', *Human Resource Management*, Vol. 28, 4 (Winter).
Kram K.E and Isabella, L.A. (1985) 'Alternatives to Mentoring: The Role of Peer Relationships in Career Development'.
La France, M. (1982) 'On Considering Aspects of the Mentoring Process', *Behaviour Today*, 19 April, pp 4–5.
Laurent, A. (1981) 'Matrix Organizations and Latin Cultures', *International Studies of Management and Organization*, Vol. 10, 4, pp 101–14.
Laurent, A. (1983) 'The Cultural Diversity of Western Conceptions of Management', *International Studies of Management and Organization*, Vol. 13, 1–2, pp 75–96.
Lawler, J. (1990) 'Mentors Can Lend an Edge', *Computerworld*, Vol. 24 (9 July).
Lawrence, P. and Spybey, A. (1986) *Management and Society in Sweden*, Routledge & Kegan Paul, London.
Lawrie, J. (1987) 'How to Establish a Mentoring Program', *Training and Development Journal*, Vol. 41, 3 (March).
Lawton et al (1981) 'When One Mentor is a Man and the Protégé is a Woman', *Harvard Business Review*.
Lean, E. (1983) 'Cross Gender Mentoring', *Training and Development Journal*.
Levinson, D. (1978) *Seasons of a Man's Life*, Knopf, New York.
Lewin, W.B. (1979) 'Mentoring: A Concept for Gaining Management Skills', *The Magazine of Bank Administration*.
Lewis, R.D. (1996) 'Wizened and Wiser', *Management Today*, May, pp 100–102.
Lorinc, J. (1990) 'The Mentor Gap—Older Men Guiding Younger Women: The Perils and Payoffs', *Canadian Business*, Vol. 63, 9.
Manz, C.C. and Sims, H.P. Jr (1991) 'Superleadership: Beyond the Myth of Heroic Leadership', *Harvard Business Review*, Vol. 19, 4.
Matthes, K. (1991) 'Corporate Mentoring: Beyond the Blind Date', *HR Focus*, Vol. 68, 11.

McCortie, C. (1991) 'Mentoring Young Achievers ', *Black Enterprise*, Vol. 21, 11.

McKeen, C.A. and Burke, R.J. (1989) 'Mentor Relationships in Organizations: Issues, Strategies and Prospects for Women', *Journal of Management Development* (UK), Vol. 8 (June).

Megginson, D. (1988) 'Instructor, Coach, Mentor: Three Ways of Helping for Managers', *MEAD*, Vol 19, part 1.

Mendleson, J.L., Barnes, K. and Horne, G. (1989) 'The Guiding Light to Corporate Culture', *Personnel Administration*, Vol. 34, 7.

Missirian, A.K. (1982) *The Corporate Connection: Why Executive Women Need Mentors to Reach the Top*, Prentice Hall, Englewood Cliffs, NJ.

Morse, M.B. (1987) 'Friends in High Places', *Success*, Vol. 34, 10 (December).

Moses, B. (1986) 'Thawing Career Freeze', *Canadian Banker*, Vol. 93, 1.

Murray, M. and Owen, M.A. (1991) *Beyond the Myths and Magic of Mentoring*, Jossey-Bass, Oxford and San Francisco.

Naisbitt, J. (1984) *Megatrends*, Futura, London.

Nasser, K. and Maglitta, J. (1989) 'Becoming an IS Mentor; Mentoring Can Be the Best Policy', *Computerworld*, Vol. 23, 47 (November 20).

Noe, R.A. (1988a) 'An Investigation of the Determinants of Successful Assignment Mentoring Relationships', *Personnel Psychology*, Vol. 41, 3 (Autumn).

Noe, R.A. (1988b) 'Women and Mentoring: a Review and Research Agenda', *Academy of Management Review*, Vol. 13, 1 (January).

Noller, R.B. (1982a) *Mentoring a Voiced Scarf*, Bearly, Buffalo.

Noller, R.B. (1982b) 'Mentoring: a Renaissance of Apprenticeship', *Journal of Creative Behaviour*, Vol. 16, 1.

Norfolk, D. (1988) 'The Female Potential', *Chief Executive* (UK).

Philips-Jones, L. (1982) *Mentors and Protégés*, Arbor House, New York.

Phillips, L.L. (1977) 'Mentors and Protégés: A Study of the Career Development of Women Managers and Executives in Business and Industry', doctoral dissertation, UCCA, Micro No. 78-6517.

Ragins, B.R. and Cotton, J.L. (1991) 'Easier Said than Done: Gender Differences in Perceived Barriers to Gaining a Mentor', *Academy of Management Journal*, Vol. 34, 4.

Ragins, M.H. (1989) 'Barriers to Mentoring: The Female Manager's Dilemma', Belle Rose, *Human Relations*, Vol. 42, 1 (January).

Reich, M.H. (1986) 'The Mentor Connection', *Personnel*, Vol. 63, 2 (February).

Roche, G.H. (1979) 'Much Ado about Mentors', *Harvard Business Review*, Vol. 57, 1.

Rogers, Beth (1992) 'Mentoring Takes a New Twist', *HR Magazine*, Vol. 37 (August).

Rubow, R. and Jansen, S. (1990) 'A Corporate Survival Guide for the Baby Boomers', *Management Review*, Vol. 79, 7.

Schneier, C.E., MacCoy, D. and Burchman, S. (1988) 'Unlocking Employee Potential and Developing Skills', *Management Solutions*, Vol. 32, 2.
Segerman-Peck, L.M. (1991) *Networking and Mentoring: A Woman's Guide*, Judy Piatkus, London.
Shapiro, E., Haseltine, F. and Rowe, M. (1978) 'Moving up: Role Models, Mentors, and the Patron System', *Sloan Management Review*, Vol. 19, 3, pp 51–8.
Sheehy, G. (1976) 'The Mentor Connection', *New York Magazine* (April 5), pp 30–9.
Sherer, Jill L. (1993) 'Elizabeth Shire's Helping Hands', *Hospitals & Health Networks* (HPT), Vol. 67, 18 (September).
Shreve, A. (1988) 'Mutual Mentors', *Working Women*, Vol. 13, 9 (September).
Smith, B. (1990) 'Mutual Mentoring on Projects: A Proposal to Combine the Advantages of Several Established Management Development Methods', *Journal of Management Development* (UK), Vol. 9, l.
Sorohan, Erica Gordon (1993) 'Wanted: (Wo)mentors', *Training and Development Journal*, Vol 47, 9 (September).
Speck, B.W. (1990) 'The Manager as Writing Mentor', *Training and Development Journal*, Vol. 44, 4 (April).
Stanley, L. (1991) 'Mentoring: What Works, What Doesn't', *Across the Board*, Vol. 28, 4.
Super, D.E. (1957) *The Psychology of Careers: an Introduction to Vocational Development*, Harper & Row, New York.
Thomas, D. (1986) 'An intra-organizational analysis of black and white patterns of sponsorships and the dynamics of cross-racial mentoring', Unpublished doctoral dissertation, Yale University.
Thomas, D.A. (1989) 'Mentoring and Irrationality: The Role of Racial Taboos', *Human Resource Management*, Vol. 28, 2 (Summer), pp 279–90.
Training and Development (1994) 'In practice', April, p. 11.
Trompenaars, F. (1993) *Riding the Waves of Culture: Understanding Cultural Diversity in Business*, The Economist Books, London.
Viator, R.E. and Slandura, T.A. (1991) 'A Study of Mentor–Protégé Relationships in Large Public Accounting Firms', *Accounting Horizons*, Vol. 5, 3.
Wade, M.N. (1987) 'How to Reactivate and Retain Employees in a Depressed Economy', *Management Accounting*, Vol. 69, 5.
Westoff, L.A. (1986) 'Mentor or Lover?', Working Women, Vol. 11, 10 (October).
White, H.L. (1990) 'The Self Method of Mentoring', *Bureaucrat*, Vol. 19, 1 (Spring), pp 45–8.
Whiteley, William T. and Pol Coetsier (1993) 'The Relationship of Career Mentoring to Early Career Outcomes', Organization Studies (March).
Willbur, J. (1987) 'Does Mentoring Breed Success?', *Training and Development Journal*, Vol. 41, 11 (November).

Wille, E. (1990) *People Development and Improved Business Performance*, Ashridge Management Research Group, Berkhamsted.

Woodlands Group (1980) 'Management Development Roles: Coach, Sponsor and Mentor', *Personnel Journal*.

Zaleznik (1992) 'Managers and Leaders: Are they different?' *Harvard Business Review*.

Zey, M.G. (1984) *The Mentor Connection*, Dow Jones Irwin, Ill.

Index

ABB Sweden 80–4
  mentoring programme 82–4
AT&T 139
Auditing process 119–20

BMG Entertainment UK 63–77
  background 64–5
  evaluation methodology 69
  evaluation report on mentoring
      66–9, 76–7
  general view of scheme 69–71
  implementation of mentoring 65–6
  interviews 69–76
  introduction and background of
      mentoring scheme 68
  objectives of mentoring 68–9
  process and matching of mentoring
      scheme 71
  responses from interviews 73–6
Brent Total Quality Programme 85
Brent Women Managers Mentorship
      Scheme 85
BT 90–2
  management development
      programme for women 90
  mentoring 91–2
Buddies 18–19
Building society, case study 115–22
Business case 2, 5, 23, 29
Business development 61

Cable & Wireless 140–1
Career counselling services 141
Career development 18, 63
Change factor, low versus high
      orientation 156–8

Change management 31, 36, 62,
      113–28
  implementing 4
  mentoring approach 114
  problems faced by addressing 113
Coach and coaching 13, 19–20, 114
  definition 18
Colgate–Palmolive 139
Commitment 57
Communication 31, 57, 61–2, 114
Communication factor, high versus low
      172–5
Communication flow 161–4
Competencies 60
  'being' 131–2
  'doing' 130–1
  international 134
Competitive edge 113
Competitive success 3
Competitiveness agenda 4
Confidentiality 15, 126
Co-option 61
Coordination of operations 62
Coordinator 28, 35
Corporate values 3
Cultural change 114
  mentoring as agent 178–9
Cultural differences
  and organizational behaviour 153–6
  applying the iceberg framework
      177–8
  dimensions affecting mentoring 155
  'iceberg factors' 155–76
  in international mentoring 153–79
  leadership styles 170–2
  potential impact 153
  status factor in 166–8

Culture, definitions   154
Culture guides   137

Data collection   118–19
Decision making   113
Development   39–58
Diagnosis of needs   46
Diversity
  development   80
  in organizations   79–99
  value of mentoring in assisting
    development of   99

Ego culture, high versus low orientation
  168–70
Élitism   2, 21, 22, 37, 80
Evaluation   36, 54–5, 66–9, 76–7, 88–90,
  105–7, 118–19, 125–7
Exercises   43

Facilitator, role of   37
Favouritism   1, 21
Feedback   28
Financial retailer, case study   122–7
Financial services sector   115

General Electric   138
Geography   57–8
Get-out clause   43, 109
Glaxo Wellcome   140
Global companies. *See* International
  corporations
Global economy   36
Global managers. *See* International
  managers
Global organizations, developing
  129–51
Globalization   115, 142
Graduate mentoring schemes   22, 23,
  25, 50, 101–12
Group versus individual orientation
  164–6
Guides   19, 46

High-potential employees, mentoring
  and developing   59–77
High-potential graduates   22, 23

High-potential managers   22, 50–1
  development, case study   63–77
Human resources managers   22

Individual learning   31
Individual versus group orientation
  164–6
Information   46
Innovation   62, 114
Integration   114
International assignments   138
  as learning experiences   134
International career action centres   141
International competence, developing
  134
International corporations   61, 129
International Distillers & Vintners
  139
International Management Cadre
  Programme   139
International managers
  'becoming'   132
  developing   129–51
  key learning issues   150–1
  long-term view of developing   133
  mentoring   136–42
  support for learning   133–4
International mentoring   129–51
  coping with time and distance   142–4
  cultural differences in   153–79
  implementing   181–4
    checklist   183–4
  key learning and questions concerning
    181–2
  opportunities, benefits and issues
    148–50
  organizational development   146–8
  self-assessment   150
International organizational
  development   146–8
Interpersonal skills development   54
Involvement, high versus low
  orientation   175–6
IT industry   36–7

Junior management as mentors   40–3

Kingfisher Management Development
  Scheme (KMDS)   102–7

INDEX

Kingfisher plc.   102–7
  evaluation of mentoring   105–7

Leadership development   31
Leadership styles   30, 153
  in different cultures   170–2
Learners   37
Learning   118–19
  and mentoring   5
  assignment-related   134–5, 137
  for the future   135
  individual   31
Learning experiences, international assignments as   134
Learning organization   5, 37, 114
Learning universe   6
Legitimacy of mentoring   158
Life-long learning   139
Line managers
  career development   63
  of mentorees   45
  supporting   53
London Borough of Brent   85–90
  aim of scheme   85
  definition of mentoring   86–7
  evaluation and learning process   88–90
  scheme and process   87–8
  target group   85–6
  target mentors   86
London International Financial Futures and Options Exchange (LIFFE)   107–12
  design of mentoring scheme   108–11
  implementing mentoring   108–12
  mentoring relationships   110
  results of graduate mentoring initiative   112
  training of mentors and graduates   111–12

Management development approach   2
Management styles   3, 4, 16, 22, 113, 153
Matching of mentors and mentorees   23–6, 66, 103, 109, 116–17, 124
MBA candidates mentoring scheme   52
Mentorees
  and change process   159
  behaviour   21
  benefits   15, 68, 70, 72, 92, 119, 126
  development   44–5
  international   144
  potential challenges   33–4
  profiles   34–5, 56–7, 124
  supporting   53
  use of term   28
Mentoring
  and learning   5
  applications   9–10
  as cultural change agent   178–9
  as extra piece of assistance   18
  as panacea?   4–5
  benefits of   119–20
  business case   2
  case studies   10–12
  challenges   122
  conclusions reached by case studies   127–8
  definition   5, 13–20, 86–7, 93, 123
  evolution   1–3
  factors contributing to success   120
  implementation   2, 3, 6, 27–37
    checklist   34–6
  in organizations   9–26
  key issues   30–1
  key learning factors   120
  key thoughts before implementing   31–2
  legitimacy of   158
  messages   45–6
  potential   1
  potential challenges   32–4
  programme design   117–18
  programme evaluation   36
  programme introduction   121
  reasons for   29–30
  relationship   1
  strategic place in organizations   3
  successful   35
  terminology   27–8
  see also International mentoring; Mentorees; Mentors; Organizational mentoring
Mentoring Contract   9, 28–9
Mentoring-management vs. organization development   1–7
Mentoring relationship   9, 14, 15, 17, 18, 22, 24, 92
  women in   98
Mentoring schemes   4, 22, 49–52
  business case and aim of   23

Index

Mentoring workshops 125
Mentors
  as change agents 158
  benefits 15, 22, 68, 70, 72, 91, 119, 125–6
  buddy-like approach 20
  definition 13
  evaluation report 67
  experience 14, 20
  external 6, 128, 138
  gender 14
  groundrules in picking 21
  half-day event 42–3
  ideal 21
  international 144–6
  junior management as 40–3
  middle management as 40–3
  potential challenges 32–3
  profiles 34, 56–7, 124, 126
  roles of 6, 14
  selecting 21
  senior managers as 24, 31, 39–40
  senior people as 23
  supporting 52–3
Mergers and acquisitions 115
Middle management as mentors 40–3
Minority groups in mentoring 98–9
Multinational companies 142

Networking 36, 56, 61
Nordson Corporation 142

Opportunity 2000 80, 85, 87, 88, 90
Organization development vs. mentoring-management 1–7
Organizational behaviour and cultural differences 153–6
Organizational development, international mentoring 146–8
Organizational learning 17, 31, 135–6
Organizational mentoring 3, 25, 30
  case study 49–52
  concept 6–7
  definition 14
  key learning points 27
  needs matrix 47
  specific 46–8
  whole organization approach 48–9

Organizational objective 16
Organizational structures 17–18
Organizations
  challenges facing 36–7
  mentoring in 9–26

Paired support relationships 18
Patronage 2
Peers 18–19
Performance competencies 60
Personal problems 17
Power base 21
Power distance, high versus low centralization 159–61
PPD (Planning Personal Development) 148
Privatization 115
Protégés 2

Questionnaire 55

Reactive behaviour 36
Research methodology 118–19
Rhône–Poulenc 139
Role modelling 23
Ruter Dam programme 80

Scandinavian Airlines System (SAS) 140
Self-assessment, international mentoring 150
Self-development 139
Self-knowledge 139
Self-managed development 37
Senior management
  as mentors 39–40
  mentoring scheme for 51
Serial mentoring 26
Shadowing 55–6
Skills coaching 18, 23
Socialization 62
South West Thames Regional Health Authority (RHA) 92–8
  benefits of programme 95–7
  definition of mentoring 93
  mentoring process 94–5
  mentors and nurses 94

    objectives of mentoring scheme   93
    post-programme developments   97–8
Sponsors   20, 99
Staff retention   59–60
Status factor in cultural differences   166–8
Strategic organizational development approach   2–4
Stress   31
Succession planning   59
Supporting mentoring   52–5

Talent spotting   62–3
Teachers   37
Technical mentors   18
Trainers   37
Training   39–58, 138
Transnational corporations   61

Transnational organization   62
Transparency   45

US Department of Agriculture   80

Videoconferencing   57

Women
    Brent Managers Mentorship Scheme   85
    BT management development programme   90
    empowerment of   88
    in management   79
    in mentoring relationship   98
    management development programme   90–1